JUMPED, FELL, OR PUSHED?

JUMPED, FELL, OR PUSHED?

How Forensics Solved 50 "Perfect" Murders

Steven A. Koehler, MPH, Ph.D., with
Pete Moore, Ph.D., and David Owen

The Reader's Digest Association, Inc.
Pleasantville, New York/Montreal/London/Singapore

A READER'S DIGEST BOOK
This edition published by The Reader's Digest Association, Inc.
by arrangement with Elwin Street Limited
Copyright © 2009 Elwin Street Limited
Conceived and produced by
Elwin Street Limited
144 Liverpool Road
London N1 1LA
www.elwinstreet.com
All rights reserved. Unauthorized reproduction, in any manner, is prohibited.
Reader's Digest is a registered trademark of The Reader's Digest Association, Inc.

FOR ELWIN STREET LIMITED
Designer James Lawrence
Project Editor Anna Southgate
Managing Editor Olivia Skinner

FOR READER'S DIGEST
U.S. Project Editor Sarah Janssen
Canadian Project Editor Pamela Johnson
Canadian Consulting Editor Jesse Corbeil
Project Designer Jennifer Tokarski
Senior Art Director George McKeon
Executive Editor, Trade Publishing Dolores York
Associate Publisher Rosanne McManus
President and Publisher, Trade Publishing Harold Clarke

Library of Congress Cataloging in Publication Data:

Koehler, Steven A.
   Jumped, fell, or pushed? : how forensics solved 50 "perfect" murders /
Steven A. Koehler with Pete Moore and David Owen.
      p. cm.
   ISBN 978-1-60652-037-6
   1. Murder--Investigation--Case studies. 2. Forensic sciences--Case
studies. 3. Homicide investigation--Case studies. 4. Evidence,
Criminal. I. Moore, Pete. II. Owen, David. III. Title.
   HV8079.H6K64 2009
   363.25'9523--dc22
                        2009018689

We are committed to both the quality of our products and the service we provide
to our customers. We value your comments, so please feel free to contact us.
      The Reader's Digest Association, Inc.
      Adult Trade Publishing
      Reader's Digest Road
      Pleasantville, NY 10570-7000

For more Reader's Digest products and information, visit our website:
      www.rd.com *(in the United States)*
      www.readersdigest.ca *(in Canada)*
      www.readersdigest.co.uk *(in the UK)*
      www.rdasia.com *(in Asia)*

Printed in Singapore
1 3 5 7 9 10 8 6 4 2

Contents

Introduction 6

1 ON THE TRAIL OF A KILLER 9

2 THE EVIDENCE EXCHANGE 45

3 GENETIC FINGERPRINTS 65

4 BLOOD, SWEAT, AND TEARS 83

5 WHAT'S YOUR POISON? 99

6 BITING THE BULLET 121

7 MAKING AN IMPRESSION 139

8 IN WRITING AND ON THE RECORD 157

Glossary 172

Acknowledgments 173

Index 174

Introduction

The investigation of an individual's death has come a long way from the days when the bodies were rapidly removed from the crime scene and detectives simply conducted a cursory examination of the area using a flashlight.

During the 1970s, the general public's exposure to the field of forensic science was the television show *Quincy M.E.* While the show solved crimes, it was a little soft on the methods of analysis that were used. Recently, shows such as *CSI, Cold Case, Crossing Jordan,* and *Forensic Files* have exposed millions of viewers to the stranger-than-fiction world of forensic death investigation, the roles of criminalists, and how analyzed evidence can be used to convict the guilty or free the innocent.

In addition, programs on Court TV have brought the public directly into the courtroom of actual high-profile cases to witness how forensic evidence is presented and challenged. Current and future criminals are also watching and learning from these programs. Therefore, those responsible for the identification, processing, and solving of crimes must always remain one step ahead.

THE ROLE OF THE CORONER

Coroners and medical examiners have a number of duties: first to determine the identity of the deceased and, second, to determine the cause and manner of death. Cases investigated include deaths that are violent, sudden, unexpected, suspicious, or medically unattended.

The task of the forensic pathologist is greatly supplemented by the highly technical skills of criminalists (or forensic science technicians) and the technology available to them at the crime laboratory. These criminalists are trained in identifying, collecting, and preserving critical evidence present at a death scene. They are also responsible for the analysis and interpretation of this evidence and presenting their conclusion in a court of law. Among the forensic scientists who visit a wide range of crime scenes on a daily basis are those searching for trace evidence. This might involve scrutinizing the surface of a vehicle for paint chips left by a vehicle during collision. Or perhaps a scientist will use a miniature suction device to remove suspect fibers from a victim's clothing. At the same time, a ballistics expert may be scouring a scene for spent cartridges, stray bullets, or the weapons themselves. Back at the lab, whole teams of forensics technicians analyze all manner of substances—from blood to semen to chemical compounds in the hope that somewhere, something will provide investigating officers with a vital clue. Through the application of scientific methodology and the combined results of the forensic autopsy and the skills of criminalists, a reconstruction of events leading up to the death may be completed, resulting in a resolution of the legal issues in question.

JUMPED, FELL, OR PUSHED?

Supplemented by an overview of the main disciplines in forensic science and the people involved, *Jump, Fell, or Pushed?* is a fascinating casebook featuring 50 real forensic cases from around the world. Spanning from the mid-1800s to the twenty-first century, each case presents an overview of the crime and highlights the forensic technique used either to put the suspect behind bars, or to prove his or her innocence.

Readers will learn how layers of different soil deposits found on a suspect's shoes helped investigating officers to reveal his true whereabouts on the day of the crime (see Steps to a Confession, p. 52); how shots fired during the course of a 911 call indicated that the crime had been premeditated and not spontaneous (see Passion or Premeditation?, p. 134); and how the relatively new science of genetic fingerprinting has proven the innocence of those who have wrongfully served long prison sentences (see Free at Last, p. 73).

A truly mesmerizing look into the world of forensic investigation, this book offers an understanding of the operations carried out by forensic scientists as they provide significant scientific information in order to convict the guilty and free the innocent.

Steven A. Koehler, MPH, PhD.

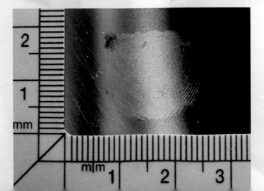

1

ON THE TRAIL OF A KILLER

Every forensics investigation starts with the scene of the crime, and a scouring of the area for evidence that may prove critical in solving that crime. From here, the investigation moves swiftly into the forensics lab, where a highly specialized team of scientists categorize and analyze everything that may be of significance—blood spatters from a wall at the scene, the remains of an interrupted meal, items of the victim's clothing—in order to determine exactly how events at the scene unfolded. Their task is aided by the careful recovery of physical evidence, the taking of accurate measurements, and photographs of all relevant data.

CASE STUDIES

- The Body in a Trunk
- The Jealous Doctor
- The Killer Con Man
- Digesting the Evidence
- Time's Up
- The Tragedy of Flight 103

Questions, Questions

While forensic science begins at the crime scene, the full extent of that scene can be difficult to pin down, and the evidence hard to find. Even in relatively straightforward cases, the forensic investigator's motto must be: Think outside the box.

A crime scene perimeter is usually taped off by investigating officers, so that access is restricted, and any evidence remains undisturbed.

WHAT CONSTITUTES A CRIME SCENE?

The red flags behind this crashed aircraft indicate the locations of human debris and sections of plane.

There may be a body on the floor of an apartment, a weapon 3 feet (1 m) away, and an apparent assailant sitting stupefied in a corner of the same room. This is the scene of a crime, but not a crime scene. The crime scene can easily be much more. Yes, it may be confined to that one room, but it could include the whole apartment or even the entire building. It may also cover the route through the city used by the murderer to reach the room, or the interior of the taxi hired by the victim to transport illicit drugs earlier in the day.

Some crime scenes are far bigger than this, even. In the case of a plane crash, for example, the place where the plane fell to earth is obviously important, but so is the path followed by the plane in the minutes before it tumbled from the air. The ground below, scattered with pieces of evidence that will help experts make sense of the incident, is just as much a part of the crime scene as where the plane landed. Likewise, the site of a road traffic accident may be in the middle of a busy highway, but the crime scene may include the half-mile of road along which the vehicles involved in the crash skidded before coming to a halt.

Alternatively, the scene of the crime may be tiny, perhaps restricted to a phone booth that can be taken away in its entirety for examination, or a computer laptop, which can be slipped into a bag.

CRIME SCENE PROTOCOL

Crimes, accidents, disasters, and other incidents that require police and forensic assistance can take many forms. Whatever the extent of the scene, however, there are some basic principles that must be followed from the moment the police arrive. The first responder—most often a local police officer—has to think fast to apply general principles to the specific situation. He or she should also be prepared to take detailed field notes, as his or her first impressions of the crime scene may be crucial to the outcome of the investigation.

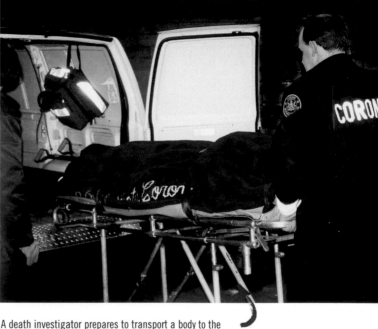

A death investigator prepares to transport a body to the mortuary in the coroner's van. The body will be examined almost immediately, before evidence is lost through decomposition.

Quick Thinking

The first responder needs to look around and take in details quickly. How many victims are there? Are the victims dead, dazed, injured, or behaving aggressively? Is the assailant still at the crime scene? The first responder's priority is to act quickly to save lives and ensure safety for everyone present, while at the same time touching as little as possible, to preserve precious evidence.

Safety First

The first responder needs to assess the situation for immediate safety according to the scene found. For example, if the scene involves a vehicle, then the first person to arrive turns off the ignition and checks for any gas leaks that could trigger a fire. If there has been an explosion in a building, then special attention needs to be given to checking for a gas leak or exposed wiring that could harm someone.

Automobile accidents are the most common death scene visited by forensic scene officers.

Body Count

Backup will probably come from paramedic teams, and the first responder keeps a record of hospitals where anyone hurt in the incident has been taken, possibly sending a police officer with the ambulances so that victims don't get "lost."

Blending in with the Crowd

Once victims are protected and cared for, there's a chance of detaining a suspect. Not every criminal flees from a scene as soon as a crime is committed. Many stick around, perhaps to cover their tracks and confuse evidence, or to commit further violence.

Preserving the Evidence

The first responder's actions aim to leave all significant evidence untampered with. Any victims are given first aid, but they must avoid washing or removing clothing, because doing so could remove splashes of blood, strands of hair, or fragments of skin that have come from the attacker.

Security Measures

Securing the physical scene is another important part of the first responder's role. As much as possible he or she should keep an eye on any exits and entrances, and note people and vehicles that have been coming and going, along with a record of the times. This information will be invaluable to the investigating team. The first responder now needs to secure the scene to avoid the deliberate or unintentional interference with physical items.

If the scene is outside, the first responder may lay a cloth or waterproof sheet carefully over evidence if it looks liable to be damaged.

Any unusual smells or strange sounds are noted. If the crime scene is in a room, it may be that someone recently there had a powerful body odor or was wearing a particular fragrance. The smell could easily have vanished by the time the rest of the team arrive, so the first responder may be the only one who has a chance of picking it up.

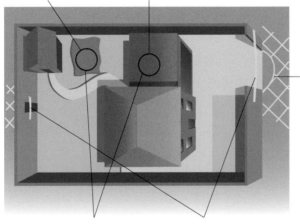

Press and unnecessary police officers are kept out, because the more people who enter the area, the greater the likelihood of contaminating the scene and destroying evidence. Also, if media reports contain too much detail of the incident, they could jeopardize a future trial. It may be that the crime scene is so open to view that police need to erect barriers to block sight lines.

There is probably a fairly well-defined primary site, but there may also be secondary sites. The first responder must identify a route in and out of these zones and, as other support personnel arrive, show them where to walk. This minimizes the chance of ruining evidence. Records are kept of everyone who arrives at, or leaves, the site.

The first responder makes sure that the area is enclosed with tape, ropes, or flags, ensuring all entrances and exits are covered. Colleagues start to take some of the load now, but these new arrivals can also contaminate the area. All visitors must wear protective overalls to avoid cross-contamination.

The Handover

Once the investigative team arrives it's time for the first responder to hand over, but the job is not completely finished. The first responder is the also first person that the crime team interviews, and is in the best position to rapidly give them the information they need to take over smoothly. The first responder makes sure his or her notes are clear while the events are still very recent, and checks any sketch maps he or she has made.

Case: ME 03-2719

A rudimentary sketch by a first responder shows the general layout of a crime scene.

A bullet casing marked off for examination. The markers have scales on them to give an indication of the size of a piece of evidence.

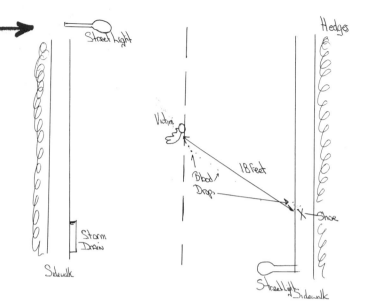

Street Light

Hedge

Victim

18 feet

Blood Drops

X Shoe

Storm Drain

Sidewalk

Street Lights Sidewalk

A knife at a crime scene, marked off for examination by forensics experts.

LOOKING FOR CLUES

With the scene secure and marked off with tape, ropes, and flags, it's time to search for evidence. A detailed sketch map is a good starting place. An officer measures the distance of items of furniture from walls, or notes parked cars, where relevant.

Initiating a Search

The investigative team must get the search right the first time, because there often isn't a second chance. Searchers disturb an area as they go over it, so the only time they can get a true impression of what the place was like when the crime occurred is the initial search. Thoroughness is combined with speed. A public street or road can't remain closed forever, and needs to be reopened as soon as possible. In addition, some types of evidence—skid marks on a road, for example—may degrade quickly. Officers must decide what constitutes useful evidence. They cannot simply pack up everything they find, so this filtering process is important. Overwhelming the forensic laboratory with too many items may result in the wrong items taking priority, or key finds getting overlooked.

The nature of the crime influences decisions about how to start searching. A murder indoors may require only a search of the room, but a bomb explosion in a shopping mall may scatter evidence far and wide. However, there are a number of general rules.

Search Basics

1. Officers start by searching any outdoor area so that evidence can't be destroyed by the weather. In addition, public places have priority because they are more difficult to secure and need to be reopened more quickly. Searches of entry and exit routes often yield more evidence than peripheral areas. If a search is needed around a body before it can be removed, then that is of high priority.

2. It is the job of the investigation team to ensure that items of evidence taken from the scene of a crime are not contaminated or tampered with in any way. For this reason, pieces of evidence need to be kept in special collection bags that reveal if anyone has ever tried to open them to tamper with the evidence. Each collection bag is accompanied by a "chain of custody" document, listing which personnel handled the item at what time, and for what purpose. Without complete documentation, a piece of evidence will be regarded as useless in court.

3. Photography plays a crucial role throughout the search phase. Forensic photographers shoot wide-angle photos of the whole scene to record general layout, and take close-ups to record exactly where individual items were discovered, the angle at which they lay, and any features of interest. They may light the scene with special flashes or other types of artificial lighting to ensure they capture as much detail as possible.

Video footage can also be useful in capturing some of the atmosphere of the location, and may help juries to get a feel of what the scene was like at the time of the crime. Court cases may occur months or years later, by which time the crime scene could have changed completely. In some investigations, images can provide the basis for experts to build a model of the scene, or a computer simulation of the event itself.

4. Very often the smallest piece of evidence can give the most powerful clue, and it doesn't get smaller than a few molecules of scent left by a fleeing criminal. No human would ever detect it, but it's easy for a well-trained tracking dog. Police investigators may also use other dogs that have been trained to pick up specific scents— chemicals used to build bombs, for example, or particles of dust that show where illegal drugs have been stored. Dogs can also be skilled in searching out human bodies or their remains by tracking and following the scent of decomposing flesh, or by sniffing for the alcohol present in particular fragrances or the aluminum compounds in some deodorants. The dogs must be introduced to the fragrance or compound before the search begins, so the investigator often requires a sample of the scent they're looking for.

PRESERVED FOR THE COURT

If an item of physical evidence is worth collecting, then it is important, where possible, to pick up a large enough sample for a battery of tests to be carried out on it. There are two main reasons for this: tests on large samples are cheaper to carry out than tests on small ones; and the defense team may well ask for part of the sample so that they can perform their own tests.

Easy Does It

When gathering samples of evidence there are some basic errors to avoid. If, for example, a doorjamb has clear marks showing where someone used a crowbar to wrench it open, and a crowbar is found lying nearby, it would seem natural for police on the scene to try to fit the two together to see if they match. But doing so would be a terrible mistake, since this would contaminate both the doorjamb and the crowbar, effectively destroying both pieces of evidence. The doorjamb along with the crowbar, should be carefully removed and both pieces of evidence should be taken away for laboratory scientists to examine.

Evidence samples must be treated correctly. They must be stored separately from one another in controlled conditions, keeping them away from sources of light and high temperatures. Some samples of evidence will require special storage conditions, including refrigeration, to be handled only by a forensics expert.

Bag and Tag

Investigating officers search any suspects detained at the crime scene, and items of interest, including clothing, are seized for later analysis. Depending on the nature of the crime, this task may be done by specialist forensic experts or a local police officer. Whoever does it, the principles remain the same. Everything is carefully bagged and documented so that investigators can use an object in a subsequent trial. Documents should include notes about the object's condition when found, and where or from whom it came. Poor documentation effectively means no evidence, because an accused person's defense team will be able to cast doubt on when and where it was collected.

Suspects and Witnesses

Suspects are, as much as possible, prevented from returning to the scene of the crime. If they were not, suspects could later claim, for example, that footprints and other apparent evidence connecting

A cadaver dog at the scene of a crime, ready to start a search. Cadaver dogs have been used by forensic experts since 1974.

them with the incident were left during visits they made immediately after the event.

Police ensure that eyewitness statements are independent of one another by keeping bystanders away from suspects and, if necessary, discouraging bystanders from talking to others about what they think happened. Witnesses talking among themselves could influence one another's memories, which would mean that nothing they say could be used in court. The investigator's job here is to ensure that if a suspect is caught and tried, defense lawyers will have little opportunity to cast doubt on eyewitness evidence.

Not everyone will be willing to act as a witness, either because they don't want to relive the trauma of the event, or they're afraid of reprisals. They may be reluctant to come forward at a later date if investigators make a plea for information. Recording names and addresses of people while they are still at the scene can give follow-up teams a much greater chance of finding them when other investigators need to get in touch.

What Actually Happened?

Revisiting a crime scene and replaying the events can help the investigation in several ways. It may shed light on how many people were involved in the event, how long different activities associated with the crime probably took, and exactly who stood where in the sequence of events. Just getting a person to walk along the route taken by a victim can jog witnesses' memories.

A reconstruction can determine whether witness statements are accurate. For example, police can find out whether people really could see particular actions given the locations they claimed to be in at the time. If the reconstruction shows that a statement is implausible, the investigators must decide whether the witness is lying, or is imagining what they think happened, rather than simply recounting what actually happened.

A good reconstruction can only take place if physical evidence at the scene has already been carefully itemized and cataloged, and analyzed alongside statements from witnesses and those involved in the incident. Without this, replaying the event is just down to guesswork, and will have limited power. Where possible, the reconstruction is staged at the same time of day as the initial event, and under similar weather conditions. If the event involved a person walking down an alley after dark, it's best to stage the reconstruction at night because, for example, the lack of light might affect the amount of time it takes to walk from one end of the alley to the other. Witnesses (or actors) take up their original positions and play out their actions to the best of their memory.

A reconstruction may also help police find more evidence. Police may use a mannequin with a hole carefully drilled to match the path taken by a bullet in the victim's body. Placing it where the victim appears to have been when shot allows investigators to shine a laser beam back through the hole and pinpoint where the assailant was most likely positioned when the trigger was pulled. Pointing the laser in the opposite direction may lead the investigators to the bullet's final resting place. Blood spatter patterns can be important, as the way that blood lands depends on the nature and sequence of different injuries.

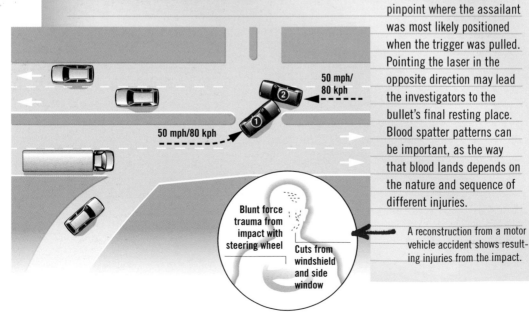

50 mph/ 80 kph

50 mph/80 kph

Blunt force trauma from impact with steering wheel

Cuts from windshield and side window

A reconstruction from a motor vehicle accident shows resulting injuries from the impact.

Under the Microscope

Scientists say that their work is "empirical," meaning that its findings and theories are based only, and entirely, on observations and recorded experience. To claim that you know something, you need to see it in some way to experience a physical event. You can have theories about how something happens, or what events occurred, but for your argument to have any strength—to be able to convict the person responsible for the crime in question—the theories need to be supported by solid evidence.

TEST CONDITIONS

Science brings with it the assumption that there is a rational world that operates according to a standard set of rules and principles. This means that a scientist can perform a test on a substance and be sure that, under the same conditions, the substance will always react in the way observed in the test. For example, an iron bar placed in water takes a certain time to rust to pieces, so a similar object placed in that sort of water will fall apart at the same rate. There are many scientists who specialize in studying the specific and universal features of the way items behave in different situations. If, for example, you take a decaying body to the correct specialist, and tell him or her some details about the place it was found and the weather conditions over the previous days, weeks, and months, the expert will be able to draw a reasonably accurate conclusion about how long the body has been decomposing.

Investigators sift through soil looking for evidence left behind by an assailant. Soil samples are often taken from areas around a crime scene for comparison purposes.

ROUTINE QUESTIONS

If a scientific assessment has been done well, then it shouldn't make any difference who performed the test. Anyone skilled in operating a particular piece of scientific equipment, and who follows agreed methods, should get the same results when they analyze a sample. The admissibility of forensic evidence in cases is based on this understanding. Both the prosecution and defense teams should get the same findings when they test any piece of evidence.

HARD EVIDENCE

"Physical evidence" includes anything that can establish that a crime has been committed or that can provide a link between crime and suspect, or crime and victim. It could be as massive as an 18-ton truck or as tiny as a grain of pollen. There are two ways in which physical evidence is useful: to identify the nature of specific items or to compare two or more samples to see if they match.

A good evidence collector will not approach a scene with a predetermined expectation of what can be found.

Identififying Samples

Criminalists can glean a huge amount of information from a tiny sample. Given a fragment of plastic, they can look at its physical and chemical characteristics and suggest what object it may have come from. Their findings can work either in favor of, or against a suspect. For example, finding that gunshot residue comes from a type of cartridge frequently used by a particular suspect for sports target practice could be important, but it would be of great interest to the defense team to discover that the residue came from a make of ammunition not used by the suspect.

Ideally, these kinds of assessments should be a matter of pure scientific evidence with no judgment needed. In reality, life is seldom that simple, and samples arriving in a forensics laboratory are often contaminated with dirt, or have degraded in some way. As a result, final decisions about samples require a fair amount of skill and experience in addition to scientific techniques.

Like for Like

Experts are also called upon to compare physical evidence, either with libraries of known samples, or with other evidence connected with

What Kind of Substances Are Tested?

- **Hair** Samples of hair may be important. Looking through a microscope at pieces of hair is often all it takes to show whether a sample has come from a human or an animal. If it is found to be human, the hair may be subjected to more technical investigations using DNA analysis to give a more detailed understanding of whom it came from.

- **Fibers** Fibers are common trace evidence, primarily because of the ease with which they transfer from one surface to another. They can be natural (wool or cotton, for example) or synthethic (rayon, nylon, and the like).

- **Drugs** Testing the composition of a white powder may show that it's an illicit or prescription drug. Scientists need to determine what type of drug it is—heroin, cocaine, or barbiturates—or a commonly used painkiller.

- **Explosives and residues** Burn marks at the site of an explosion may reveal particles of specific explosives or the chemicals they normally leave behind. The examination of gunshot residues on hands and around gunshot wounds can point to a particular gun or incriminate a suspect.

Today's forensic experts have an armory of tests for finding out more about specific substances such as hair (top), drugs (center), and gunshot residue (bottom).

the crime. The question here is whether two or more of the samples came from the same place. This can be resolved by seeing if a sample recovered from a crime scene matches samples collected from a suspect or victim. A match could confirm that a suspect was at the scene, while finding that the hair couldn't have come from the suspect tells you that either he wasn't there or that you have a second suspect to consider.

Comparing physical evidence is a two-stage process. In the first, the forensic scientist performs a range of tests on the samples. In the second, investigators form an opinion of whether the results indicate that the two samples have a common origin.

Despite the advances made by DNA technology, finger-printing remains vital to a crime investigation. No two fingerprints are alike.

Finding a Definite Match

Making these comparisons often comes down to a question of probability—what's the likelihood of the apparent match happening by chance? Juries may be faced with an expert witness testifying that there is a one-in-a-million probability that a particular match occurred by chance. The information can appear compelling, but defense lawyers will remind jurors that the chance of winning a lottery jackpot is often set at odds of around one in 14 million. The fact that in most weeks someone does win shows that even highly improbable coincidences can occur.

The forensic scientist's task is to find a set of tests that show that the chance of a random match is unlikely. This means looking for aspects of a sample that vary widely within a population, but are fixed within a single person or object. Where a characteristic can point to a definite link with next to no doubt, it's called an "individual characteristic," and includes the following:

- **Fingerprints:** This is one of the classic examples of individual characteristics, as there is virtually no chance of two people ever having identical prints—not even identical twins. Comparing a fingerprint collected at a scene with one taken from a suspect in a police station is a powerful way of using physical evidence.
- **Bullet striations:** Matching the scratches on a bullet with imperfections in the barrel of a gun is a convincing way of linking a firearms offense to an individual weapon.
- **Footprints:** Crimes have been solved by looking at the fine detail of the tread on a person's shoes and matching it to footprints found next to a victim.

Casting a Wider Net

All too often, this tight link between the two samples of evidence proves elusive, so forensic investigators need to look further. Information can be gained by looking at the "class" of an item. An empty cigarette pack found near the victim, for example, could be the same type that a suspect is known to smoke. On its own, the evidence doesn't link the suspect to the crime, but it's one clue that can add to any assessment of the probability that this person was at the scene.

GI-1   C 11

1

Comparing a test bullet (left) and a bullet found at a crime scene (right) can identify the weapon likely used.

Data from this type of evidence (known as circumstantial evidence) has the advantage of being free from personal bias—it simply exists—and interpretation becomes a matter of assessment; the decision ultimately rests with a jury. The problem here is that, once again, faced by a seemingly infallible forensic scientist, juries may give too much weight to an individual piece of evidence. There is, after all, a world of difference between saying that a piece of physical evidence indicates a possibility that the suspect and a particular item of evidence are linked, and saying that the two are definitely tied together. However, circumstantial evidence can form a web of connections that eventually catches the fly.

Crossing the Boundary

The problem with circumstantial evidence is its imprecision, since it does not identify any one person, while individual evidence does exactly that. Sometimes improvements to methods of analysis give more accurate information about an item of evidence, so that the item changes categories. For example, blood samples used to be divided into classes according to blood types (A, B, O, AB). This division was useful, but millions of people share the same blood type

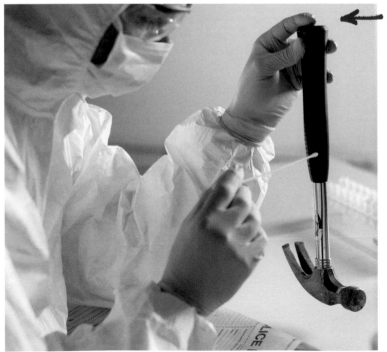

A forensic scientist examines a potential weapon. Forensic experts look for, and analyze, evidence, recording their findings in detail.

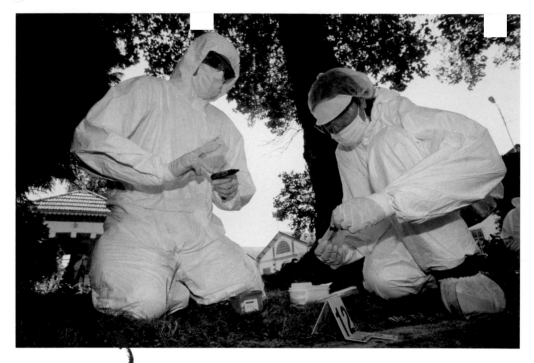

Forensics officers at work at a crime scene, collecting the marked evidence. Crime scene investigators wear full protective suits to prevent contamination of the scene.

so it was imprecise. With the advent of genetic technology, experts can now look at the DNA makeup of cells within each sample. This type of evidence points with much greater precision to an individual person. Blood smears can now be individual, rather than class, physical evidence.

The point at which an item of physical evidence crosses the boundary from being a piece of circumstantial evidence to a piece of individual evidence is difficult to assess and is often argued between forensic scientists and police investigators. An outcome to an investigation can come down to a question of extensive background research to determine the likelihood of two items matching, even though they come from different sources.

The issue is not only how many identical items there are, but also the chance of that item being found in a particular location. Looking at the pack of cigarettes again, a tobacco manufacturer makes millions of packs of a brand of cigarettes every year. Just finding a pack could indicate that one of thousands of people could have dropped it.

If, however, the pack was of an unusual brand of Brazilian cigarettes and was discovered at the scene of a crime in Scotland, then the finger of suspicion would point more strongly at a businessman or -woman who, perhaps, made frequent journeys to South America and was known to smoke cigarettes.

Back at the Lab

Forensic science is a huge industry. Today there are literally hundreds of public crime laboratories to assist police at the town, city, and state or province level. Having said that, there is also no such thing as a standard forensics laboratory.

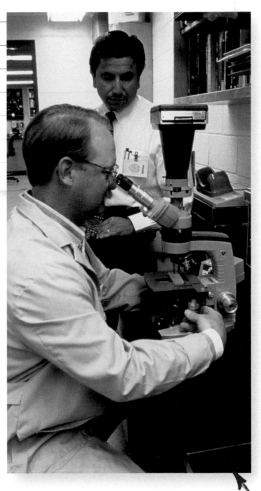

A detective and a lab technician use a microscope in the forensic laboratory to review evidence from a crime scene.

Some large, city-based labs are attached to universities, police departments, or directly linked to the coroner's office. Others are independent agencies working for a range of clients and may employ dozens of people, all working in particular specialties. By contrast, a laboratory that serves a small town may be run by a single scientist and packed with numerous pieces of equipment. The scientist sends off pieces of evidence to specialist consultants, effectively creating his or her own team.

A forensics laboratory looks drab and uninspiring: white-boxed lumps of technology stand on a scrupulously clean floor or sit on work stations bereft of personal touches. The excitement lies in the laboratory workers' ability to combine a wide range of machines, skills, and experience to glean valuable data from the most unpromising samples.

Whether it is large or small, every forensic lab needs to implement the following two standard procedures:

1. The contamination of samples must be avoided. If a blood smear found at a crime scene and a blood sample taken from a suspect somehow come into contact with one another, any findings are of no forensic value, so a laboratory needs to run management systems that ensure such an event can never happen. If evidence is documented, collected, and stored in the correct manner, it can often be presented in court years after the criminal act took place.

2. Every lab must have a rigorous method of recording evidence, including keeping track of who has examined it (chain of custody), when each examination occurred, and what tests were carried out. This is important as one test may influence the validity of any subsequent observation on the sample.

A FORENSICS ROLL CALL

Crime labs are often divided into a number of sections or units.

- **Physical science unit** This unit takes techniques developed in chemistry, physics, and geology and applies them to pieces of evidence. In a large laboratory, the physical science set-up may be

A forensic scientist studies the results of a DNA test on a sample taken from the scene of a crime.

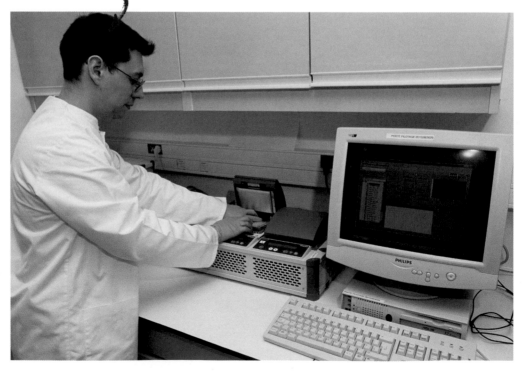

subdivided into teams that specialize in individual materials, such as paints, explosives, or soils.

- **Biology unit** This unit has a massive focus on analyzing DNA, as this is a powerful marker that can link individuals with a crime, while exonerating other suspects. This unit also analyzes plant samples and microscopic trace evidence, such as pollen or bacteria, which can give investigators vital clues in piecing together events surrounding a crime. A subsection of the biology unit will focus solely on extracting information from blood. (See also Genetic Fingerprints, pages 64 to 81)
- **Toxicology unit** The forensic toxicologist deals with the harmful effects of chemicals on humans. While it is forensic analysts who perform the actual testing of biological samples, to identify and quantify the amount of the chemical present, toxicologists determine the relationship between the exposure to a chemical and the noxious effects on the body. These chemicals may have

The Federal Bureau of Investigation (FBI) serology laboratory in Washington, DC, where samples of blood and body fluids are analyzed.

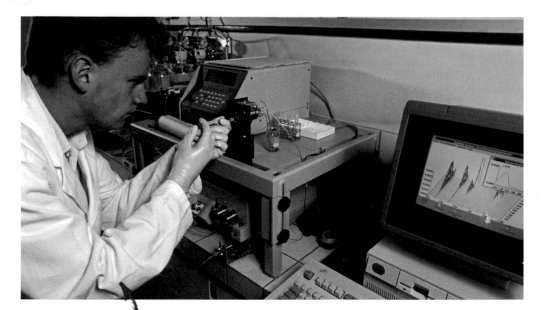

A forensic toxicologist analyzes evidence from a crime scene for traces of drugs using a gas chromatograph.

been ingested, injected, or absorbed by the skin, and they may have been taken either deliberately or accidentally, or in some cases administered to a person without their knowing, in cases of deliberate poisoning. Methods for drug screening range from a simple spot test (where a reactive chemical is used to test for a particular suspected substance) to highly sensitive and sophisticated screening methods such as gas chromatography and mass spectrometry. (See also What's Your Poison, pages 98 to 119)

- **Photographic unit:** These specialists are called on by other units to help record evidence before it is examined, as well as during its examination. Forensic photographers use specialized films and lighting to reveal information that the human eye can't see.

- **Entomology unit:** The forensic entomologist is specially trained in the life cycles of insects, as well as methods of identification, preservation, and how these facts can be used to determine the time of death of an individual. Not all bodies are discovered shortly after death. A number are found in advanced stages of decomposition. Literally moments after a death, flies arrive on the body to lay their eggs. The maggots that emerge can be used to determine the time the eggs were laid and therefore the estimated time of death.

- **Firearms unit:** Ballistics experts are kept busy by the frequent misuse of guns. Examiners are called upon to determine the operational level of a weapon, to test weapons, to describe the features of bullets and cartridges, to compare bullets and

A policeman fires a pistol retrieved from a crime scene at a paper target. The casing from the bullet fired here will be analyzed in the firearms unit to see if it matches casings taken from the crime scene.

cartridges from one scene to another, and to conduct gunshot powder residue testing. This unit has firing ranges for testing weapons, and microscopes for scrutinizing bullets and shell cases. It may also have its own equipment for analyzing chemicals and gunpowder residues, or may outsource this to the physical science unit. (See also Biting the Bullet, pages 120 to 137)

• **Fingerprint unit:** Crime novels love to concentrate on the fingerprint unit in a laboratory although, because most criminals are now well aware of the need to wear gloves, this is not always the busiest section. Even so, many crimes are not carefully planned, in which case fingerprints can become valuable means of showing who has been present at a crime scene. (See also Making an Impression, pages 138 to 155)

• **Document examination unit:** This unit becomes involved in a huge range of crimes, from passport forgery to murder. These specialists draw on many different skills, including analyzing the chemicals in ink and working out the sorts of marks that different printing techniques leave on paper. (See also In Writing and on the Record, pages 156 to 171)

• **Epidemiology unit:** The newest field to emerge in forensics, this concerns documenting detailed statistics about the dead—fatality trends and the emergence of new drugs, for example.

Testing, Testing

A large part of the work of a forensic laboratory is identifying the material that makes up a piece of evidence. This could be because investigators need to know exactly what it is, or because they want to use this information to compare two or more samples. Scientists have a massive array of tests that can help provide answers to two different questions. What sorts of material are present in a sample? And how much of each type of material is present? In analyzing a drug sample, for example, the first analysis could tell you that there is some ecstasy and some talcum powder, the second would tell you the proportion of each. Both assessments have their uses in different situations.

- **Chromatography:** A process used to identify chemicals as different as dyes, drugs, and residues found in dirt. It can also identify genes, proteins, and DNA from tiny samples. A number of different methods exist, all based on a similar scientific principle of treating a substance in such a way that its various components separate out and can therefore be identified.

- **Electrophoresis:** A process that uses an electric current to separate different-sized molecules in proteins, which can then be taken for further analysis. Blood and semen are some of the substances that are run through this test in order to determine a genetic fingerprint.

- **Spectrometry:** A process used for analyzing the different components of a sample after separation, which it does by testing its light absorption and reflection qualities. Using a spectrophotometer, experts can see exactly which colors of light are affected by a sample, and then compare this information with samples of material that they already know about.

- **Mass Spectrometry:** A process that uses high-energy electrons to knock electrons out of the sample molecules, causing the molecules to fall to pieces. The mass spectrometer then uses a magnetic or electrical field to measure the mass of each piece. A particular molecule will always break into the same range of pieces, and there is next to no chance that two different molecules will break into the same sets. Therefore, an experienced forensic specialist should be able to take a sample of material and tell exactly what chemical it is.

- **Neutron Activation Analysis:** A process that looks at the heart of the atoms in a sample, exposing it to gamma rays, before determining what atoms are present. It can tell whether atoms of particular elements are present right down to levels as low as one part per billion. Forensic scientists use it to detect trace elements in metals, drugs, paint, soil, gunpowder, and hair.

- **X-ray Diffraction:** A process used to determine the atomic structure of a substance, in which X-rays are fired at a sample, colliding with its atoms and bouncing off, onto a sheet of photographic paper. The way the X-rays bounce is set by the nature of the atoms they strike; every material produces a unique pattern on the photograph—a unique diffraction pattern.

Dr. Kim Rossmo

Professor and Geographic Profiler, Vancouver Police Department, Vancouver, Canada

A DAY IN THE LIFE

There are only a few geographic profilers in the world, all from major police agencies, so I often travel to far-flung places to provide assistance in cases of serial murder, rape, bombing, and arson. Today is the first day of my visit to a city I have never seen before.

By the time I leave, I will have visited places most lifelong residents won't even be aware of—nor want to.

12 NOON I meet with the detectives of the case, gathered around a conference table in the task force headquarters, coffee cups in hand, as we know will be working until the early hours of the morning. Because geographic profiling is relatively new, I start with a presentation on its theory and methodology, capabilities and limitations.

2:00 P.M. It's time to hit the streets. We visit the locations connected to a serial murder case, viewing the victim-encounter and body-dump sites. My goal is to answer questions related to how the offender hunted for his victims, why he knew these areas, what is his comfort zone, and—most critically—where he lives.

The attacks of even the most bizarre serial killer are hardly ever random.

During the visit to the crime sites, I look for geographic clues: street routes, arterial roads, jogging paths, transit lines, and late-night bars. Geographic profiling analyzes crime locations to determine the most likely area of offender residence. It cannot solve a crime (only physical evidence, a witness, or a confession can

do that), but it can help investigators manage information and prioritize suspects. Other techniques, such as DNA testing, can then be more efficiently applied. Because geographic profiling is an investigative support technique, I rarely go to court. Underlying this work is an extensive body of research on human behavior and the geography of crime. So it is not surprising that I often work closely with psychological profilers. They provide the "who," and we provide the "where."

6:00 P.M. We break for a short while. As the murders in this case happened at night, our visit needs to be repeated in the dark.

11:00 P.M. We reconvene, again to trace the path of the killer. There is always an underlying pattern to how the killer hunted for his or her victims and where he or she chose to commit the crimes. By decoding that pattern, I hope to help investigators find who they are looking for. This may take several days. Once I have all the evidence I can find, I will conclude my visit by preparing a preliminary geoprofile for the investigators, and will conduct a brainstorming session on possible investigative strategies. On return to my office, I will sit down and prepare a thorough written report.

CASE STUDY: The Body in a Trunk

VICTIM Toussaint-Augsent Gouffé
CAUSE OF DEATH Strangulation
WHERE Paris, France
WHEN July 27, 1889

The Crime

On July 27, 1889, a Parisian debt collector named Toussaint-Augsent Gouffé was reported missing. On August 15, a road worker passing through the hamlet of Millery, south of Lyon, noticed a terrible smell rising from the bushes along the riverbank. There he found a badly decomposed body, tied up in a cloth. The corpse was taken to the morgue in Lyon, but there was nothing to reveal its identity. When the find was reported to M. Goron, the head detective of the Paris police, he thought it might be Gouffé, and the missing man's brother-in-law went to identify the remains. He did not recognize the corpse, but as its hair and beard was black, it could not be Gouffé, who had bright chestnut-colored hair. Two days later the remains of a cabin trunk were found nearby, also smelling of decomposition, with a label showing it had been sent by train from Paris to Lyon on the day Gouffé had been reported missing, and a key found near the body fitted the lock.

The Case

The corpse was already buried when Goron visited Lyon, but the pathologist had kept some of the victim's black hair; when this was rinsed in distilled water, the black dissolved, revealing a natural chestnut color. Goron was then able to have the body exhumed and reexamined. A defect of the right knee, together with a missing tooth and an old ankle injury, proved it was Gouffé. It also showed he had been strangled.

But who had killed him? One of Gouffé's work colleague revealed that another person with links to the bankruptcy world, Michel Eyraud, had disappeared from Paris at the same time with his mistress, Gabrielle Bompard. The police reassembled the trunk and put it on show in the city morgue. At the end of the year a letter arrived from a boardinghouse keeper in London, who said that Eyraud and Bompard had stayed there in July. In addition, it was revealed that two people matching their descriptions had bought a trunk in a shop there before returning to France.

Scenes taken from an illustrated account of the Gouffé mystery.

The Evidence

In January 1890, Goron received a letter from Eyraud in New York, protesting his innocence and blaming his former mistress. The very next day, Bompard reported to the Paris police, but merely put the blame on Eyraud. She was arrested and agents were sent to track down the missing Eyraud, who was eventually discovered in Havana and brought back to Paris to appear before the trial judge on July 1, 1890, almost a year after the murder.

The couple admitted they were destitute, and had planned for Bompard to lure a victim to a secluded apartment where they would kill and rob him. They couple found a basement apartment in the Rue Tronson-Ducoudray and, on their London visit, bought the trunk, a pulley, a length of rope, and some canvas, which Bompard sewed into a bag to contain the corpse. The pulley was fixed to a cross beam above the bed, and they chose their victim with care. Eyraud and Gouffé had a friend in common who revealed that on Friday nights Gouffé would try to pick up a woman to spend the night with. This would make it fairly easy for Bompard to lure him to the apartment. There Eyraud would hide behind a curtain, and when Gouffé was distracted he would slip the rope around his neck, and haul him up over the pulley until he was throttled.

The Outcome

The murder went according to plan, but they found little of value on the corpse. Eyraud went to Gouffé's office but missed 14,000 francs hidden under papers. All they could do was strip the body, place it into the bag, and lock it in the trunk. It was then sent to Lyon where they collected it, dumped the body and the trunk, and fled to America before it was discovered. Each blamed the other for the decisive role in murdering Gouffé. Bompard was finally sentenced to 20 years in prison, and Eyraud was executed.

CASE STUDY: The Jealous Doctor

VICTIMS	Isabella Ruxton and Mary Rogerson
CAUSE OF DEATH	Strangulation
WHERE	Moffat, Dumfriesshire, Scotland
WHEN	September 29, 1935

The Crime

On the morning of Sunday, September 29, 1935, Susan Haines Johnson was walking over a stone bridge across a stream called the Gardenholme Linn, north of the small Scottish town of Moffat, when she happened to look down into the gully. There she saw a bundle, out of which protruded a human arm. Over the following eight days the police investigation uncovered a succession of other body parts, including two heads. Later on, two more bundles were found by the roadside in the area. All the badly decomposed fragments were taken to the Anatomy Department of the University of Edinburgh where they were to be reassembled in a bid to establish their identities.

The Case

It was clear that cutting up the bodies so completely must have been a long and complex procedure, as the culprit had gone to great lengths to obscure the victims' identities; fingerprints had been chopped off, the genitals had been removed, as had the facial skin along with ears, eyes, noses, and lips, and several teeth had been extracted. Such efforts would have required a detailed anatomical knowledge and must have taken around eight hours to complete. Investigators were able to establish when the parts had been dumped by the stream, as they were wrapped in newspaper dated September 15, two

weeks before their discovery. In addition, a heavy rainstorm four days later would have washed away the bundles, so police began searching for people reported missing over that brief period. Eventually they found a newspaper report that the wife and maid of a Lancaster physician, Dr. Buck Ruxton, had both vanished on September 14. After hearing reports of Ruxton's extreme jealousy toward his wife Isabella and his increasingly erratic behavior, police decided to search his house.

The Evidence

More evidence began to emerge: part of the newspaper wrapping turned out to be a particular edition of a national paper sold only in the towns of Morecambe and Lancaster, and a local newspaper vendor confirmed that a copy had been delivered to Ruxton's home on September 15. The head of one of the victims was wrapped in a set of child's rompers that had been passed on by the maid's mother for the Ruxtons' children. Finally, a search of the house revealed bloodstains and traces of human fat in the drains. On October 13, Ruxton was arrested for the murders of Isabella Ruxton and the maid Mary Rogerson. In the meantime, the bodies had been reconstructed as far as possible given the degree of mutilation, and both the height and the age fitted those of the missing victims.

Much more conclusive though, was the information that was missing from the bodies, as numerous identifying marks and features had been removed from the bodies of the two women in the dissection process: Mary had had a squint and her eyes had been removed from her corpse; she'd had a birthmark on her arm and skin had been cut away from the site of the mark; an appendectomy scar had also been cut away as had a scar at the base of her thumb. Isabella's prominent teeth had been removed, as had her large nose. Then, through new and innovative forensic techniques, experts were able to superimpose a photograph on an image of her skull and found it a perfect fit. Finally, another expert studied the development of maggots in the body parts found on the riverbank and was able to show that both victims had died at about the time Isabella and Mary were last seen alive.

The Outcome

Dr. Ruxton was charged with both murders, and the overwhelming body of evidence convinced the jury, who found him guilty of both killings. He was executed on May 12, 1936. In a written confession, released after his death, he claimed that he had killed his wife in a fit of jealous rage, but that the maid had witnessed the murder, sealing her fate as his second victim.

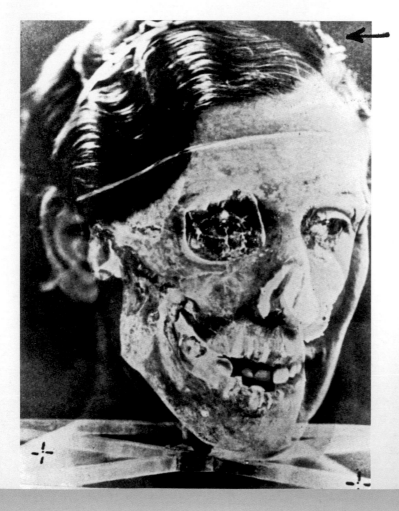

A portrait of Isabella Ruxton superimposed onto one of the skulls found at the scene of the crime.

CASE STUDY: The Killer Con Man

VICTIM Olivia Durand-Deacon
CAUSE OF DEATH Probable gunshot wound
WHERE Crawley, Sussex, England
WHEN February 1949

The Crime

As a victim's body so often plays a crucial role in helping to identify his or her killer, some murderers try to escape detection and conviction by placing the body out of reach of investigators. John George Haigh was a successful and professional con man who charmed a succession of wealthy but lonely women into giving him money. Unfortunately, this created a disposal problem since, once he was successful, his lifestyle depended on being able to move on to find the next victim while at the same time evading arrest for his previous crimes. His solution was to kill his victims, and he decided the best way to dispose of their remains was to dissolve each body in a bath of sulfuric acid to destroy all evidence before it could be used against him.

The Case

The case that brought about his downfall began in February 1949, when Constance Lane and Haigh himself, both residents of the Onslow Court Hotel in South Kensington, London, reported that another resident, wealthy 69-year-old widow Olivia Durand-Deacon, had vanished. Haigh said that he had been due to meet her to discuss a business proposition at his workshop in Crawley, Sussex (where he worked using strong acids to break down industrial materials), but claimed she had never arrived. When police interviewed hotel staff they discovered that Haigh owed money to the hotel and that he kept close company with several elderly and wealthy women. When they visited his workshop, they found containers of acid, a cleaner's receipt for a Persian lamb fur coat, which belonged to Durand-Deacon, and a recently fired Enfield revolver. Then, to their surprise, Haigh calmly admitted that they would never find the missing woman's body, as he had destroyed it with acid, leaving only a completely untraceable sludge. How could the police prove murder with no body?

The Evidence

Intent on convicting Haigh, investigators returned to his workshop, and found large quantities of sludge in the yard outside. It contained a tiny pebble-like object that they were able to identify as a human gallstone, together with fragments of partly dissolved bones, and a set of plastic dentures that was largely undamaged. The dentures were matched to those of the victim after checking with her dentist. The bones were identified as human, from the spine, legs, and feet, and in addition the foot and anklebones showed clear signs of severe osteoarthritis, a condition from which the victim had suffered, according to Durand-Deacon's family. Police also reconstructed the surviving foot and took a plaster cast, which fitted one of the victim's shoes perfectly. Blood splashes on the wall of the workshop were consistent with the victim having been shot while she was bent over a workbench, possibly studying business papers.

Other evidence found in the sludge included a strap from a handbag the victim was carrying on the day she disappeared, and the rest of the bag was later discovered hidden in the workshop yard. Experiments carried out with an amputated human foot and the body of a sheep showed, by the rate they were dissolved by concentrated sulfuric acid, that the body in the acid had been there since the day of the victim's disappearance. Other witnesses testified they had seen Haigh and the victim together on the afternoon she had vanished, though he returned alone to London that night.

The Outcome

The full story emerged step-by-step after the identification of the remains at the workshop. It seemed that Haigh, a chronic and unsuccessful gambler, was so short of cash that he had tried to interest his wealthy victim in a project to make and sell fake plastic fingernails. In the meantime, he bought large quantities of sulfuric acid and stored them at his workshop. On the day after Mrs. Durand-Deacon vanished, he visited two jeweler's shops, one to sell her watch and the other to have items of her jewelry valued. Finally, when charged with her murder, Haigh admitted five other killings. He was put on trial and the jury was so unimpressed by his assertion that without a victim's body he could not be convicted, that it took just 15 minutes to find him guilty of Durand-Deacon's murder. He was hanged at Wandsworth Prison on August 6, 1949.

John George Haigh smiles as police lead him, handcuffed, to his trial on April 1, 1949.

CASE STUDY: Digesting the Evidence

VICTIM Lynne Harper
CAUSE OF DEATH Strangulation
WHERE Goderich, Ontario, Canada
WHEN June 9, 1959

The Crime

On the evening of June 9, 1959, 14-year-old Steven Truscott was seen riding his bicycle along a lane leading away from the Royal Canadian Air Force base at Goderich, near Clinton, in Ontario. Sitting on the crossbar was a classmate, 12-year-old Lynne Harper. Around 7:00 P.M. that same evening, the pair were seen by another witness near a small thicket known as Lawson's Bush, though a third witness passing by the area a few minutes later reported that he had seen no sign of them there. Lynne was never seen alive again.

It was not until two days later that her body was found—partially hidden by trees in Lawson's Bush. She was lying on her back, partly undressed, and had been strangled with her own blouse. Because of a continuing period of hot weather, her body had already begun to decompose, but a pair of footmarks found between her feet, which bore the imprint of crepe rubber soles, suggested she had been raped. Investigators were able to confirm this at her postmortem. However, an analysis of her stomach contents showed a partly digested meal suggesting she had died before 7:30 P.M. at the latest, just 30 minutes after having been seen with Steven Truscott.

The Case

When questioned by police, Steven Truscott said he had arrived home at 8:30 P.M., an hour after Lynne's

estimated time of death. He claimed to have dropped Lynne off at the nearby main road, where he had seen her get into a automobile, specifically a gray Chevrolet with U.S. license plates. Since no one else had seen this vehicle, and it did not accord with where Lynne had been found or her time of death, no one believed his story.

The Evidence

Truscott was arrested and given a medical examination. There were abrasions on his penis, which suggested he had recently had sex with a degree of force, though he claimed these were the remains of a recent rash. He also had a scrape on his left leg, his pants were torn, and careful washing had failed to remove grass stains on the knees. Furthermore, Truscott was known to have a pair of crepe rubber-soled shoes, though these could no longer be found. Though the evidence was highly circumstantial and lacked any definite proof that he had murdered Lynne, he was convicted and sentenced to death, though this was commuted to life imprisonment on account of his age.

The Outcome

Because of the lack of solid evidence and his model behavior as a prisoner, Steven Truscott was granted leave to appeal against the sentence in 1967. The

Steven Truscott, arriving at a news conference on August 28, 2007, the day his conviction was overturned.

grounds for the appeal rested on different estimates of what the state of Lynne's stomach contents could reveal about her likely time of death. One school of thought was that the normal processes of digestion could be held up by strong emotions or physical violence. This would render the relatively undigested meal almost irrelevant as an indicator of the time of death, which could have been at any time before her body was found in the two days that had elapsed since her disappearance. Had this been the case, it might have been possible that she was attacked and killed by the occupant of the mysterious Chevrolet

elsewhere and dumped not long before she was found, which would have put Steven Truscott out of the reckoning. Others disagreed, saying that the girl had been murdered at that spot, not just brought back and dumped there.

It was not until August 2007 that Truscott's case was finally declared a miscarriage of justice, based on new forensic evidence. An examination of maggots that had been found on the victim's body in 1959 suggested that the eggs had been laid early in the morning of June 10. Since this usually happens very shortly after death, it was highly unlikely that Truscott was the killer after all.

CASE STUDY: Time's Up

VICTIMS Five members of the List family

CAUSE OF DEATH Gunshot wounds

WHERE Westfield, New Jersey, United States

WHEN November 1971

The Case

The murders were discovered on December 7, 1971, when police went to investigate why lights were ablaze in the Lists' large Victorian house, night after night, even though they were away on vacation. In the mansion's large ballroom they found the bodies of Helen List, and the couple's daughter and two sons, each one neatly laid out on a sleeping bag and all having suffered gunshot wounds. In the small upstairs apartment was the corpse of List's mother, Alma, who had also been shot. List had left letters that explained he had killed his family to protect their souls from corruption by the world's increasing moral breakdown. His automobile was found in a JFK Airport parking lot but there the trail ended. As the years passed, it seemed he had escaped justice.

The Crime

Recent forensic science developments, such as the reconstruction of facial features from skulls of long-dead victims, or retrieving DNA samples from skeletal remains, have brought killers to justice after years, or even decades, have passed since their crimes were committed. For example, New Jersey accountant John List, who vanished after killing his wife, their three teenage children, and his mother, in November 1971, was captured and charged with his crimes after 18 years of evading justice.

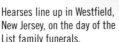

Hearses line up in Westfield, New Jersey, on the day of the List family funerals.

The Evidence

After his dramatic escape, a vast amount of publicity featured List's picture, but no sightings were reported. The only person who thought she might have seen him was a Wanda Flannery, living in Aurora, Colorado. She read an article on the murders in *Weekly World News* magazine in February 1987, and noticed that List closely resembled one of her neighbors, named Robert Clark, who lived with his wife, Delores. She spoke to Delores about the resemblance, but an angry rebuttal calmed Flannery's suspicions and the matter was dropped. In the following year, the Clarks moved to Richmond, Virginia.

In the meantime, Captain Frank Marranca, who had been appointed head of the Major Crimes Unit in Elizabeth, New Jersey, approached the producers of a popular television series, *America's Most Wanted*, which had proved successful in tracking down several criminal fugitives. As the producers were concerned at the lack of a recent picture of John List, forensic sculptor Frank Bender was called in to produce a likeness of List after 18 years. This time, they would not be working from a skull, but with a computer program that had been devised to simulate the effects of aging. An expert criminal profiler, Dr. Richard Walter, was asked to assess the effects of List's attitudes and lifestyle to determine how his appearance might have changed over the years, and to advise the computer specialists which factors to use in running the program.

He decided List's religious background would rule out radical plastic surgery, that his avoidance of exercise would cause him to put on weight, and that his need for eyeglasses would have developed into having to use larger and thicker lenses as he grew older. All these factors were used in generating a new image as the basis for a sculpture, which was used in the televised reconstruction of the crime, broadcast on May 21, 1989. John List normally watched the show, but missed that episode as he and Delores were at a church social. But Wanda Flannery saw it.

The Outcome

More than 300 phone calls resulted from the show. The one that finally brought an end to List's escape was from Wanda Flannery's son-in-law, who gave them the Clarks' new address in Richmond, Virginia. Two FBI agents checked out the lead, and "Robert Clark" was arrested and finally put on trial under his original identity for the murders of his family. After a seven-day trial, he was found guilty on April 12, 1990, and given five life sentences. List died, still serving his sentences, on March 21, 2008.

Retired police chief James Moran and his wife Evelyn, 1989. Moran holds a copy of the FBI's "Wanted" poster of John List.

CASE STUDY: The Tragedy of Flight 103

VICTIMS 270 people
CAUSE OF DEATH Airplane bombing
WHERE Lockerbie, Dumfries, Scotland
WHEN December 21, 1988

The Crime

At just after 7:00 P.M. on the evening of December 21, 1988, a Pan American Boeing 747 was flying at 31,000 feet (9,448 m) over western Scotland en route from London to New York, when its echo disappeared from ground control radar screens. The huge aircraft broke up in midair and the largest pieces fell onto the small town of Lockerbie below, where they hit the ground with the force of a minor earthquake. In all, 259 people aboard the aircraft and 11 people on the ground died in the tragedy.

The Case

Fragments of wreckage were spread across a huge area of the Scottish countryside, in two distinct trails. The first step in determining the cause of the aircraft breaking up was to collect as many pieces as possible. It was an enormous task, tracing more than four million fragments of wreckage spread over approximately 1,000 square miles (2,590 square km). All were brought to a reassembly hangar in a military depot near Carlisle, Scotland, for reconstruction, fitting each part of the aircraft into the right relationship with its neighbors in the 747's structure.

From the beginning, investigators found worrying anomalies. The pieces of the aft baggage hold had fallen in a fairly restricted area, whereas those of the forward hold were far more scattered, suggesting

this had been one of the first parts of the aircraft to break up. This implied a bomb may have been placed in the hold, and when two of the cargo containers placed in the forward hold showed clear signs of explosive damage, the suspicion was confirmed. Then came the discovery of a tiny fragment of printed circuit board, forced into a crease of the container paneling by the blast of the explosion. It was traced to a particular model of Toshiba radio/cassette player, and must have contained the explosive. Other fragments showed the device had been hidden in a brown suitcase, which had been loaded into the container so that it was against the plane's outer skin.

The Evidence

The aircraft parts were sent to the Royal Aircraft Establishment in Farnborough, England, for a full three-dimensional reconstruction to determine the breakup sequence. For example, the noise of the bomb exploding was heard on the cockpit voice recorder moments before a complete power failure stopped the recording. And parts of the cables that held the curtains screening the baggage container were found in one of the engine air intakes, showing that the forward fuselage had burst open while the engines were still running normally.

To determine the amount of explosive involved, armament experts placed different amounts of explosive in identical cassette radios and detonated them in identical luggage containers. Through comparing the damage with the explosive damage shown by the containers aboard the aircraft, they were able to deduce that just 2.2 pounds (1 kg) of explosive had been enough. In determining who was responsible for the disaster, the rest of the investigation was a triumph of forensic detection—the position of the cassette in the hold showed it had been transferred from a connecting flight from Frankfurt before Flight 103 had taken off from London. Clothing fibers also found in the luggage were traced to items bought in Malta and flown to Frankfurt the day before, and inquiries on the island later traced them to unnamed Libyans.

Holland at a special court, held under Scottish laws, representing the country where the victims had died. On January 31, 2001, after a nine-month trial, Al Amin Khalifa Fhimah was acquitted but Abdelbaset Ali Mohmed Al Megrahi was found guilty of the murders and he was sentenced to life imprisonment, to be served in Glasgow's Barlinnie Prison.

The Outcome

Finally, a case was brought against the Libyan intelligence services, and under pressure of economic sanctions, the Libyan government identified two of their agents, Al Amin Khalifa Fhimah and Abdelbaset Ali Mohmed Al Megrahi, as the men responsible. They were put on trial in

The fuselage of Flight 103. Investigators assembled the pieces to make a complete reconstruction of the plane so they could determine how the blast could have happened.

2

THE EVIDENCE EXCHANGE

Any encounter between two individuals (or an individual and the environment) results in an exchange in physical material—be it a strand of hair, particles of synthetic fibers, soil traces, or flecks of paint. No matter how much care a criminal takes, such traces are invariably left behind at the scene of a crime, at which point trained experts meticulously collect them for investigation. Often too small to be seen by the naked eye, these tiny items take on a new significance when observed with a microscope, and can become key evidence in bringing a criminal to justice.

CASE STUDIES:
- Steps to a Confession
- Kiss and Makeup
- Blundering Train Robbers
- Trapped by Trace Evidence
- Clues in the Ruins
- Road Rage
- The Soccer Shirt Murders
- Telltale Paint Traces

Hairs, Fibers, and Flakes

The more careful a criminal has been, the more observant an investigator has to become. At a crime scene, an investigator may go over the area using a miniature vacuum cleaner fitted with flat filter discs that are regularly replaced and transferred to a sealed, labeled plastic bag. Investigators may choose to lift hairs, fibers, and flakes from a small area by grabbing them on the back of a strip of sticky tape, or by removing the object the sample is lying on and taking it back to the controlled conditions of a laboratory, where experts can scrape or wash it.

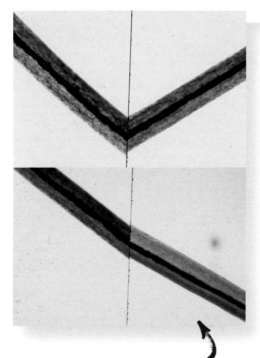

A hair from a suspect and one found on a victim are viewed under a comparison microscope. The image at the bottom shows no match, while the top image shows a positive match.

A HAIR'S BREADTH

It's difficult to stop hair falling from your body. A few strands fall from your head each hour, and if an assailant struggles with his victim, there could easily be strands lodged underneath a fingernail, or bound in with clothing. In the case of the Blundering Train Robbers (page 54), a single hair was found stuck to a button on one of the suspect's overalls. Although this alone was not enough to convict him, along with other evidence it contributed to building a picture of the man.

A strand of hair can indicate a person's sex and give a tentative assessment of their age.

During a forensic investigation, hair traces may undergo the following procedure:

1. **Retrieval:** Strands of hair at a crime scene are picked up with forceps and placed in clip-top bottles. In cases of rape, medical staff use a clean comb to recover any foreign hairs from the victim's pelvic region and also take samples of the victim's own hair to act as controls. Investigators may want to pluck up to 50 hairs from each body region of interest from any suspect so that they have a good range of hair for comparison. On occasion, evidence collectors may collect hair from a hairbrush found in a suspect's room.

2. **Comparison:** Back at the lab, a criminalist uses a comparison microscope to analyze strands of hair taken from the crime scene and strands from a suspect. The expert places one strand on the microscope stage and another strand on an adjacent stage. Through the microscope's single viewfinder, both strands can be viewed at high magnification, comparing color, diameter, and features of the medulla (the middle of the hair shaft). By studying the scales that line the exterior of each sample strand, experts can see if the hair strands are similarly arranged.

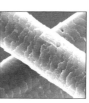
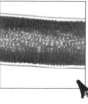

   Although this process allows an expert to judge how similar the two strands are, it can't prove a definite link to an individual person. There's too much variation in hairs from an individual, and too much similarity between people. But hair comparison is still very valuable. To start with, while it may not prove a link between crime scene samples and a suspect, it can sometimes conclude that the strands found by evidence collectors did not come from a particular individual. This may help police rule out particular people from their investigation.

A cross-section of hair fiber (left) shows its compostion of medulla (central core), cuticle (outer layer), and cortex (the layer between the two). Human hair (top right) is distinguishable from animal hair (bottom right) in the root, medulla, pigmentation, and scales.

3. **Characteristics:** Hair analysis may help form a theory about the suspect's racial background—because hair characteristics often vary with race—or may reveal where on the body the hair came from (armpit hair is oval in cross-section, beard hair is triangular, head hair is round, and eyelashes taper rapidly to a point). Looking at the hair root can indicate whether it had been pulled out during a violent struggle or fell out naturally. An examination of the hair shaft can indicate whether it was cut. If there is no root, careful microscopic examination of the cut ends may show what sort of implement had been used. Viewing it with different lights and with

spectrophotometry may show if it has been dyed or bleached, which can give a clue about the owner.

4. **Drugs** A strand of hair can be used as a form of biological diary. If someone takes an illicit drug, for example, a small amount of that drug lodges in the millimeter of hair that forms in an average day. Analyzing sections of cut hair using mass spectrometry will give an indication of patterns of drug use, as well as revealing clues about diet and exposure to industrial or environmental chemicals.

5. **Other traces** Hair can also carry other evidence such as traces of dust or blood, fine fibers from fabric, or small particles of paint.

LOOSE FIBERS

Like hair, natural fibers such as cotton and wool vary greatly within a single sample, and so can't be used definitively to link a crime scene sample to a suspect. But the machine-made uniformity of synthetic fibers means that analyzing synthetics in clothes, seat covers, and carpets can give much more conclusive and valuable results. For example, when investigating the disappearance of two young girls in

Animal Fur

Fur may look similar to human hair, but microscopic examination and careful measurement show that the two are very different. Most fur is finer than human hair, and different species of animals have different characteristic scale patterns on the exterior of the strand. Although finding strands of fur may occasionally help solve a murder or other serious crime, fur is more often significant in cases of animal trafficking, or where law enforcement officers are looking for evidence of misuse of animals in the production of food, clothing, or accessories.

Fibers analyzed using a process called colored scanning electron micrograph (SEM) are found to be those of an animal.

Soham, England (see page 62), police discovered 154 fibers from their soccer shirts in and around the suspect's home, confirming their suspicions that his version of events was not true.

There's a wide range of chemical and physical analyses that can be carried out to characterize a synthetic fiber, and all this information can be used to compare a sample from the crime scene with one taken from a suspect.

Synthetic fibers may undergo the following procedures:

1. **Physical makeup** The physical makeup of a fiber is noted—whether it is natural or artificial—and what shape or diameter it has. Further analysis will give an indication of the number of filaments in a single strand, how big they are, and how many times they have been twisted over a certain length. If the fiber has been dyed, which is often the case, the type of dye used will also be analyzed.

2. **Chemical composition** The chemical composition of a fiber can often be assessed using mass spectrometers, chromatography, or heating the fiber and measuring its melting point. Like hair samples, synthetic fibers may be coated with fragments of other evidence that can be collected and analyzed.

3. **Post-crime inspection** Because they are so small and light, fibers can float in the air for hours and even days. This means that investigators often return to a crime scene a few days after the initial inspection to see if any new fibers have settled. On occasion, crimes have been solved after an investigator has searched through the filters in an air-conditioning unit and found fibers linked to a suspect who claimed never to have been in the building. Looking for these sorts of lodging places can be particularly useful if the crime occurred a few days, weeks, or even months before anyone was aware of it, and the search teams arrive after the area has been disturbed or cleaned.

Analysis of fibers taken from a crime scene shows that they are from the strap of a bra, and are composed of nylon and polyester.

A TRACE OF PAINT

A burglar uses a crowbar to force open a window and enter a property. He wears gloves so as not to leave fingerprints, and is careful enough not to leave any other evidence such as footprints, blood, hair, or fibers. How do police link this crime with a particular suspect? Paint chips might provide the answer. This was certainly the case when police investigating the death of a South Korean student in London (see page 63) discovered paint traces that led them to their chief suspect, not only for the murder of this student, but for that of a second South Korean student as well.

Paint traces undergo the following procedure:

1. **Sample match** The police know that tiny chips of paint from the crowbar-damaged surface of the windowsill probably attached themselves to the burglar's clothing as he climbed through. Criminalists take paint samples from the window and try to link these with chips of paint from the suspect's clothing. If the two pieces of evidence match, there's a strong probability that they both came from the same place.

2. **Layering** Paint samples can be particularly useful in solving vehicle crimes since the paintwork is often made up of many layers. Police keep databases of compositions and color ranges used by large vehicle manufacturers. Investigators look at the layering of the flecks under a microscope. Paint is usually applied in three or more layers. A link can be inferred if the examination shows that the samples have identically ordered layers; the possibility of this happening by chance is very small. Also, manufacturers change their formulas frequently, so if a chemical analysis of the paint compares with paints listed in the databases of manufacturers' formulas, a batch of paint can be located in place and time.

In another case, while examining a chip from an automobile under a microscope, an expert may notice that the top layer is more loosely bound to the surface than preceding layers, a good indication that the vehicle has been repainted. The police now know to look for a repainted automobile.

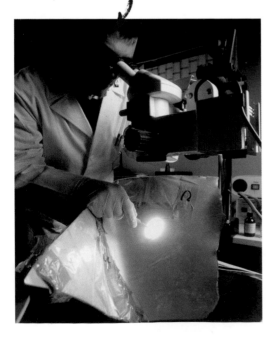

A forensic scientist uses a microscope to collect a paint sample from part of an automobile, following a collision with another vehicle.

Dr. Shaun Ladham

Forensic Pathologist, Allegheny County Coroner's Office, Pennsylvania, United States

One of the fascinating aspects of my job is that it is so varied, I never know what type of case I will be investigating on any particular day. Listening to the newscast on the way into work a murder is reported, but little detailed information is given.

7:45 A.M. It's usually quiet when I arrive at the office—the deputy coroners are settling into their 7:00 A.M. to 3:00 P.M. shift, and the receptionist's desk is still unmanned—but today, the place is buzzing. Two police murder detectives meet me in the lobby. I ask if they are here for the case reported on the news. They nod and say it's bad. I quickly change into scrubs and walk to the autopsy suite with them.

8:00 A.M. I pick up the paperwork for the case, which includes the death investigation report, and read the following: "The victim is a 6-month-old white female, who was discovered in her bedroom by police after day-care workers became concerned when the little girl was not dropped off at 6:00 A.M. this morning and there was no answer at the residence. At 6:15 A.M., police arrived at the residence, entered, and located the girl DOA. A quick examination of the scene revealed trauma to the head region. A search of the room failed to locate any object out of place or with blood on it. The core body temperature of the victim was 97°F (36°C) and the ambient air temperature was 78°F (26°C)."

10:00 A.M. I examine the photographs taken by the death investigators at the scene. The room is a typical little girl's bedroom, apart from the blood spatter on the bed and the ceiling. I call the forensic science lab and am told that the criminalists are still processing the crime scene. The detectives inform me that the girl lives with her father at this home on weekdays and at her mother's home during the weekend. The parents are married, but are involved in a tumultuous divorce. No records of past domestic problems are on file with either the police or childcare agencies.

11:30 A.M. After reviewing all the information, I proceed with the postmortem examination. The girl is removed from the cooler and placed on the autopsy table. Even with my years of experience and having performed thousands of autopsies, I am not always prepared for such brutal and senseless deaths as this.

12 NOON As I examine the little girl, I determine that she was killed by multiple blows to the head with a hammer-like object. I instruct the detectives to return to the scene to search for the weapon. My rage at this senseless killing has to be tempered if I am to conduct a thorough, objective, and complete examination. If not, I could miss critical evidence that might create a problem for the district attorney during subsequent criminal proceedings. The worst part is that, in several months, I will have to relive this experience during my testimony at the murder trial.

CASE STUDY: Steps to a Confession

VICTIM	Margarethe Filbert
CAUSE OF DEATH	Strangulation
WHERE	Rockenhausen, Bavaria, Germany
WHEN	1908

The Crime

The body of Margarethe Filbert was found near the village of Rockenhausen in Bavaria. The local prosecutor was intrigued by the discovery of some hairs gripped in the victim's hands, and called in Frankfurt forensic scientist Georg Popp, who had achieved a successful conviction in a similar case four years before.

The Case

In this case, Popp was able to confirm the hair was a false clue, as it belonged to the victim herself. He did discover, nevertheless, that the principal suspect was a local farmer and factory worker named Andreas Schlicher, who had earlier been suspected of minor crimes like poaching. However, Schlicher denied having been anywhere near the murder scene on the day of the crime.

The Evidence

Popp found that Schlicher's wife had cleaned his dress shoes on the night before the murder, and that he had worn them only on that day. When Popp examined them, with the help of a geology specialist named Fischer, he found soil and other materials trapped between the sole and the heel, which must have been deposited on the day of the murder. For comparison, he took a series of soil samples from the field where the body had been found, from around the suspect's home, from the surrounding fields, and from a ruined castle where the suspect's rifle, ammunition, and spare pants had been found, despite his denying having been there.

When he removed the soil deposits from beneath Schlicher's shoes, he found several distinct layers had been stuck to them in sequence, which enabled him to reconstruct the suspect's movements on the day of the murder. First a layer of soil with fragments of goose droppings had been picked up around his home, then grains of red sandstone showed he had been in the fields where the body had been found. Finally, soil containing coal and brick dust, and cement powder, showed he had visited the ruined castle in spite of his denials. At the same time, the complete absence of porphyry (milky quartz and mica with root fibers), leaves, and weathered straw showed that he had not spent any time walking around the fields of his own farm, as he had claimed when questioned.

The Outcome

Though Schlicher had maintained his story through prolonged questioning, Popp's meticulous reconstruction of his movements left him dumbfounded, and he confessed to having murdered Margarethe Filbert. Once again, Popp's logical and painstaking microscopic analysis, long before advances like DNA, had identified a killer and succeeded in producing an admission of guilt.

CASE STUDY: Kiss and Makeup

VICTIM Marie Latelle
CAUSE OF DEATH Strangulation
WHERE Lyon, France
WHEN 1912

The Crime

When Marie Latelle was found to have been murdered at the home of her parents in 1912, suspicion fell on her boyfriend, Emile Gourbin, who was thought to have killed her in a fit of temper. However, Gourbin appeared to have an iron-clad alibi, as he had been playing cards with friends at the time that Latelle had been killed.

The Case

The Lyon Police Laboratory had been established by Dr. Edmond Locard, formerly Assistant Professor of Forensic Medicine at the University of Lyon, who now ran the forensic service. He had already produced his now-famous theory that "every contact leaves a trace," so that in a murder there would be evidence of the victim found on the person of the killer, and traces of the murderer found on the victim, or at the crime scene. These traces might include fingerprints, footprints, bodily fluids, skin fragments, and hairs.

The Evidence

Locard began by examining the body of the victim, who died from strangulation. He then went to visit Gourbin in his cell and took samples from beneath his fingernails. These included skin fragments but, so long before advances like DNA, there was no chance that these could provide a positive evidential link to the individual victim. However, Locard searched the minute samples very carefully for any other traces that might yet establish guilt. Under the microscope, he found the skin fragments were coated with particles of a pink dust, which were analyzed and identified as rice starch. Even closer analysis showed these particles were coated with the most minute traces of bismuth, zinc oxide, magnesium stearate, and a reddish iron oxide pigment known as Venetian red.

This complex mixture was almost certainly face powder. In those days, before cosmetics were mass-produced, it was common for women to buy face powder from their local pharmacist, who would make it from their own individual formula. Locard searched every pharmacist's shop in the city, to find out which ones produced cosmetics, and which formula they used. Of all the premises he visited, only one mixed up this formula for face powder—the one patronized by Marie Latelle.

The Outcome

When Gourbin was confronted with the evidence, he confessed to the murder of Marie. He also admitted to having altered the time on the clock in the room where the card game had taken place, to mislead his friends that it was later than it really was. This gave him his alibi, suggesting that he had left the game after Marie was killed when, in fact, he was on his way to kill her.

French criminologist Dr. Edmond Locard.

CASE STUDY: Blundering Train Robbers

VICTIMS Three members of the Union Pacific train crew and a mail clerk.

CAUSE OF DEATH Gunshot wounds

WHERE Ashland, Oregon, United States

WHEN October 11, 1923

scent from police tracker dogs, a battery and detonator used to set off the explosives, a revolver, and a single pair of overalls. There was nothing, it would seem, to indicate who had carried out the brutal attack.

The Crime

When an attempt was made to rob a Union Pacific mail train in the mountains of Oregon in 1923, it seemed at first that, although the criminals responsible had panicked and fled after killing the train crew and blowing up the mail coach—yet before seizing any of the loot—they had at least been careful to leave nothing that could lead to their identification. Detectives searching the scene of the crime found only a pair of shoe covers that had been soaked in creosote in an attempt to blot out their

The Case

The criminals could hardly have been more wrong. Edward Heinrich, in charge of the forensic science laboratory at Berkeley in California, subjected the overalls to a detailed examination, and came up with an astonishing amount of information on the person who had worn them. Traces of grease had been found on the material, leading police to suspect they had belonged to a garage mechanic, but Heinrich analyzed the substance in detail and revealed it came from pine trees. Small chips of Douglas fir

Portraits of the D'Autremont brothers, from left to right: Hugh, Roy, and Ray.

were also found on the overalls, together with a hair stuck to one of the buttons, strands of tobacco, and nail clippings, and a tiny piece of folded paper almost destroyed by having been washed while in a pocket of the overalls.

The Evidence

To the skilled investigator, this evidence resulted in the identification of the anonymous owner of the overalls: the hair found on the button of the overalls showed he was a fair-haired man in his 20s, while the size of the overalls suggested he was some 5 feet 10 inches (178 cm) tall and weighed between 154 and 168 pounds (70 and 76 kg). The tree grease and chippings suggested he worked as a logger, the tobacco revealed he rolled his own cigarettes, and the nail clippings that he was unusually careful about his appearance. He was identified as being left-handed by the differences in wear patterns on the overalls, which showed he buttoned them from the left, while the pockets on the left-hand side showed greater wear than those on the right.

But the clinching piece of evidence was the tightly rolled, matted piece of paper. It was carefully unwrapped and treated with iodine to bring up the original printing, whereupon it proved to be an evidential gold mine. It was a receipt from the U.S. Post Office for a registered package for one Roy D'Autremont, living in Eugene, Oregon, in the heart of the heavily forested region of the northwest. Police then checked the address and spoke to neighbors, who confirmed Roy matched all the descriptions produced by the forensic laboratory, but that he had disappeared, along with his brothers Ray and Hugh.

The Outcome

The police drew up descriptions of the other two brothers, and all three were posted as wanted men. At first it seemed the trail had died out, but four years after the robbery, a U.S. Army sergeant serving in the Philippines said Hugh D'Autremont was serving in his unit. He was arrested in Manila, after which his brothers were tracked down to an Ohio steel mill, where they were working under false identities. Confronted with the evidence against them, all three confessed to the crime and were sentenced to life imprisonment.

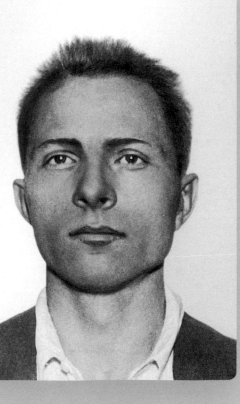

CASE STUDY: Trapped by Trace Evidence

VICTIM Graeme Thorne
CAUSE OF DEATH Strangulation and beating
WHERE Bondi, Sydney, Australia
WHEN July 7, 1960

The Crime

In the 1960 Sydney Opera House lottery, Bazil and Frieda Thorne bought ticket 3932, which won them a prize of 100,000 Australian pounds when the lottery was drawn, on June 1. Thorne was a successful traveling salesman and the family had managed to send their eight-year-old son Graeme to a highly regarded private school, Scots College. Each weekday morning he would walk from the family home in the Sydney suburb of Bondi to get a ride from the mother of two of his classmates a block away. But on Thursday, July 7, 1960, he disappeared. The family's sudden and well-publicized new wealth had made him the victim of the first child kidnapping for ransom in Australia's history.

A handcuffed Stephen Bradley arrives at Sydney Coroner's Court on December 6, 1940 during the inquest of Graeme Thorne's death.

The Case

The Thornes reported their son's disappearance, and police sergeant Larry O'Shea was in the house when the kidnapper rang, demanding 25,000 Australian pounds by 5:00 P.M. that day or the boy would be killed. The man spoke with a thick East European accent, and said he would call back later with orders on how the ransom was to be paid. The second call never came, but a massive media campaign helped to produce pieces of evidence. Graeme's school case, cap, lunch box, coat, and math books were found scattered along a busy highway leading to the seaside town of Seaforth. But the boy himself was not found until August 16, when children found a bundle hidden under a rock ledge on a Seaforth vacant site. It contained the eight-year-old's body, still dressed in school clothes and wrapped in a blanket. He had been bound hand and foot, strangled, and beaten to death.

The Evidence

In the meantime, neighbors had told investigators that they had seen a blue 1955 model Ford Customline on the morning of the abduction, close to where Graeme had vanished. Police had embarked on the huge task of checking owners of every vehicle matching the description. News coverage of the discovery of the body brought a call from William and Kathleen Telford, who lived in Clontarf, the next suburb to Seaforth. They told police that their neighbor, Steven Bradley, had this type and color of automobile, but he seemed to have gone away. The police questioned Bradley at work, but he denied all knowledge of the abduction. They released him while they searched for more evidence, only to find that he, along with his wife and three children, had left for England on the passenger liner *Himalaya*, and his automobile had vanished altogether.

More evidence was uncovered from Graeme's body. There were traces of mold on his shoes and socks, cypress seeds and animal hairs on his clothing, and some unusual pink grains. The development of the mold at the time the body was found showed that he must have died at about the time he was kidnapped, while the animal hairs were found to belong to a Pekinese dog. The pink grains were from an unusual type of mortar used in house construction and the cypress seeds were from a variety that was not found where the body had been left.

The Bradleys' house, however, matched all the evidence. It had pink mortar between the bricks, the right type of cypress in the garden, as well as a photograph showing a family picnic on the very blanket used to wrap Graeme's body. The missing automobile was finally tracked down to a used automobile dealership, where a search revealed traces of pink mortar in the trunk, and the Bradleys' missing Pekinese dog was found in a veterinary hospital.

The Outcome

Australian police were sent to Sri Lanka, where the *Himalaya* was due to pause on its voyage. After convincing the initially skeptical Sri Lankan authorities of the strength of their case, they brought the family back to Australia. Stephen Bradley was tried for the murder of Graeme Thorne, convicted, and sentenced to life imprisonment.

CASE STUDY: Clues in the Ruins

VICTIMS	168 victims
CAUSE OF DEATH	Bomb explosion
WHERE	Oklahoma City, Oklahoma, United States
WHEN	April 19, 1995

The scene of destruction after the bombing of the Alfred P. Murrah Federal Building in Oklahoma.

The Crime

On April 19, 1995, the multistory Alfred P. Murrah Federal Building in the center of Oklahoma City was blown apart by a massive bomb, killing a total of 168 people, many of them children in a day-care center within the building.

The Case

With such a huge explosion on their hands, investigators were set the challenge of having to search for evidence amid thousands of tons of rubble and wreckage. On this occasion, though, they had the extraordinarily good fortune to find a vital clue early on in the process, with the discovery of a piece of twisted metal. It was identified as part of the axle of a van—almost certainly the vehicle that had carried the bomb. Even more encouraging was the fact that the part carried a partial vehicle identification number, which enabled the van to be traced. When investigators checked in the vehicle database maintained by the National Crime Insurance Bureau, they found it was a 1993 Ford, operated by Ryder rentals company, and that this particular vehicle had been rented from the company's Junction City, Kansas, branch.

The Evidence

Finding the people who had rented the van required straightforward detective work. Ryder staff at Junction City helped police produce sketches of the two men who had rented it and teams of investigators began interviewing staff at all the hotels, restaurants, diners, and gas stations between Junction City and Oklahoma City to see if anyone remembered seeing either man. Lee McGown, manager of the Dreamland Hotel in Junction City, recalled seeing one of the men depicted, who had signed the register as Timothy McVeigh, a different name than the one used to rent the van. On the assumption that this was his real name, police started to track him down, only to find he was already under arrest. A highway patrol officer had flagged down McVeigh's battered yellow Mercury Marquis because of a missing license plate. McVeigh was found to be trying to conceal a semiautomatic pistol, and he was put under arrest and taken to Noble County Jail. The Michigan address shown on his driver's license was checked and found to be the home of Terry Nichols, who became the second suspect. Bomb experts estimated the damage done to the building would have taken some 4,000 pounds (1,800 kg) of a mixture of ammonium nitrate fertilizer and fuel oil, both of which are easily obtainable ingredients. Fragments of the barrels that had held the explosive, found at the site of the explosion, had markings similar to barrels found at Nichols's home, and traces of the explosives were found on the clothing of both suspects.

The Outcome

Timothy McVeigh and Terry Nichols were put on trial for the Oklahoma City bombing. In June 1997, McVeigh was found guilty on all charges and sentenced to death by lethal injection. Nichols, who was seen as an accomplice rather than the prime agent for the killings, was given life imprisonment. McVeigh's lawyers mounted a succession of appeals, all the way to the U.S. Supreme Court, but all proved unsuccessful and he was executed on June 11, 2001, in a federal prison at Terre Haute, Indiana.

McVeigh took part in an interview while in prison, June 23, 1995, in Oklahoma City.

CASE STUDY: Road Rage

VICTIM Lee Harvey
CAUSE OF DEATH Knife wounds
WHERE Bromsgrove,
West Midlands, England
WHEN December 1, 1996

The Crime

Returning home from an evening in a pub at Bromsgrove, in the West Midlands, on December 1, 1996, Lee Harvey and his girlfriend, Tracie Andrews, were apparently the victims of an appalling case of "road rage." At around 11:00 P.M., having passed a dark-colored Ford Sierra containing two or three men, this vehicle then tailgated them, flashing its headlights, until it managed to pull in front, forcing the couple to stop. When Harvey got out to confront the driver, he was subjected to a frenzied knife attack, during which he was stabbed over 30 times. His girlfriend was hit in the face by one of the attackers before the automobile sped off and emergency services were called. Harvey died without regaining consciousness.

Tracie Andrews, shown shortly after the incident, bearing the marks of having been hit in the face.

The Case

After a huge search to try to find this automobile and its occupants, police became worried by unexplained gaps appearing in Andrews's story. One witness, Susan Duncan, who had arrived on the scene just after the attack, said she had not heard another vehicle driving away from the scene, as did other local witnesses. By this time more and more people were revealing the constant fights between the couple; one witness had seen them behaving angrily toward one another on the evening of the murder, while police records showed that, following complaints by Andrews, they had intervened on one occasion.

The Evidence

While in hospital following the attack, Andrews made half a dozen visits to the bathroom before she was searched and interviewed. By the time suspicions had been aroused, it was too late to retrieve whatever she might have dumped; the bin for clinical waste and hand towels—

Bloodstains found in the suspect's boot linked her directly to the crime.

a perfect hiding place—had already been emptied. However, a thorough search of the murder scene uncovered a tiny spring and a pair of tweezers, identified as part of an imitation Swiss Army knife. The autopsy showed that this type of knife could certainly have produced the wounds suffered by Harvey. Although the weapon itself was not found, an examination of Andrews showed a complex blood pattern inside the top of her boot, and this corresponded with the blade of such a knife; she could have hidden it there until she was able to dispose of it.

The Outcome

Six months later, Andrews was charged with Harvey's murder. She was found guilty and sentenced to life imprisonment. Her intention to appeal her conviction was rejected, and she later confessed to the crime.

CASE STUDY: The Soccer Shirt Murders

VICTIMS Holly Wells and Jessica Chapman
CAUSE OF DEATH Probably asphyxiation
WHERE Soham, Cambridgeshire, England
WHEN August 5, 2002

The Crime

In the Cambridgeshire village of Soham, two 10-year-olds, Holly Wells and Jessica Chapman, vanished on Monday, August 5, 2002. They were last seen at 6:30 P.M., walking through the village. The last person to see them alive was school caretaker Ian Huntley.

The Case

Police searched potential hiding places, including Huntley's house. Both house and automobile were scrupulously clean, and a cell phone expert revealed that the girls' phones had probably been switched off outside the residence. Under police questioning, Huntley's girlfriend, Maxine Carr, claimed she had been upstairs in the bath when he had briefly spoken to the girls outside the house. Initially unaware of Huntley's checkered record of violence to women and sex with underage girls, police soon discovered his full history.

The Evidence

A more thorough search of Huntley's house revealed a key to a storage shed at Huntley's workplace. Inside, police found burned items of the girls' clothing in garbage bags covered with Huntley's fingerprints. The following morning, on August 17, Huntley and Carr were arrested, and later that same day the mystery of the girls' fate was tragically solved. A couple, walking in the countryside near Lakenheath Royal Air Force base northeast of Soham, noticed the appalling smell of rotting flesh. When they looked for the source, they found two small bodies dumped in a waterlogged ditch.

Police found Huntley's hairs on the clothing fragments in the garbage and, although the automobile's tires and trunk lining had been changed, they found ten red fibers from the girls' soccer shirts inside the vehicle. In all they found 154 fibers from the girls' clothing inside the house. Finally, they found mud and pollen grains on the vehicle's underside, which perfectly matched conditions at the site where the girls' bodies had been left. Faced with increasing forensic evidence, Huntley finally changed his story.

The Outcome

Huntley admitted that the girls had come to the house, asking after Maxine, when Holly suffered a nosebleed. Huntley had been washing his dog in the bathroom and had tried to stop the bleeding when Holly had slipped and fallen into the bath. Jessica had started screaming that he had pushed her, and to keep her quiet he had put his hand over her mouth only to find she had suffocated, by which time Holly, too, was dead. The jury didn't believe his version of events and found him guilty of the girls' murders. He was given two life sentences, and in September 2005, his minimum prison term was set at 40 years.

CASE STUDY: Telltale Paint Traces

VICTIMS	Hyo Jung Jin and In Hea Song
CAUSE OF DEATH	Suffocation
WHERE	Yorkshire and London, England; and Toronto, Canada
WHEN	November 2001 to 2002

The Crime

On November 9, 2001, a suitcase abandoned in a hedge bordering a country lane in the village of Askham Richard, near York, England, was found to contain the partly clothed body of a young Asian woman, her face tightly bound with adhesive tape. Forensic experts took fingerprints, examined her teeth, and checked her DNA but could not identify her. Only when details went to Interpol was a link established, through a Pacific-based missing persons website, to official South Korean government citizen records. These included fingerprints, which finally produced a match for a 21-year-old South Korean student called Hyo Jung Jin, who had vanished on a brief visit to England, after finishing a course in French Literature at the University of Lyon, France. She was traced to an address in West London, but apart from the fact that she had slowly suffocated because of the tape over her mouth, there was nothing to show who was responsible.

The Case

Coincidentally, another female South Korean student, In Hea Song, had disappeared from London in early December. Her body was found three months later, hidden in a cupboard in a house in East London. Like Jin, she had slowly suffocated—her nose and mouth sealed with adhesive tape. It emerged that both of the properties involved were owned by the same landlord, Kyo Soo Kim, who had been living in the West London house at the time Jin had vanished. Following the disappearance of the second student, Kim had moved to Toronto, Canada, but was arrested on a brief trip to London, while the search for evidence began.

The Evidence

The first link was the parcel tape used to suffocate Jin, which matched that of a partly used roll found in the West London house, stained with Kim's blood. Blood was also found on the walls, carpet, and baseboards, but this matched that of Jin, as did blood samples found in the trunk of an automobile that was hired by Kim in October 2001. Blue paint found on one corner of the suitcase also matched blue paint on one of the bedroom walls.

Items found with Song's body showed traces of Jin's DNA, though a different tape had been used to suffocate her. A search was also made of Kim's house which revealed a T-shirt, splashed with orange paint, and which provided a perfect match with orange paint traces on the tape used to bind Song's wrists; traces of Kim's own DNA were also found on the garment.

The Outcome

The detailed forensic evidence added up to a watertight case, placing Kim at the scene of both murders and linking him directly with the attempts to conceal the bodies. He was put on trial and, on March 25, 2003, was found guilty of both murders and sentenced to life imprisonment.

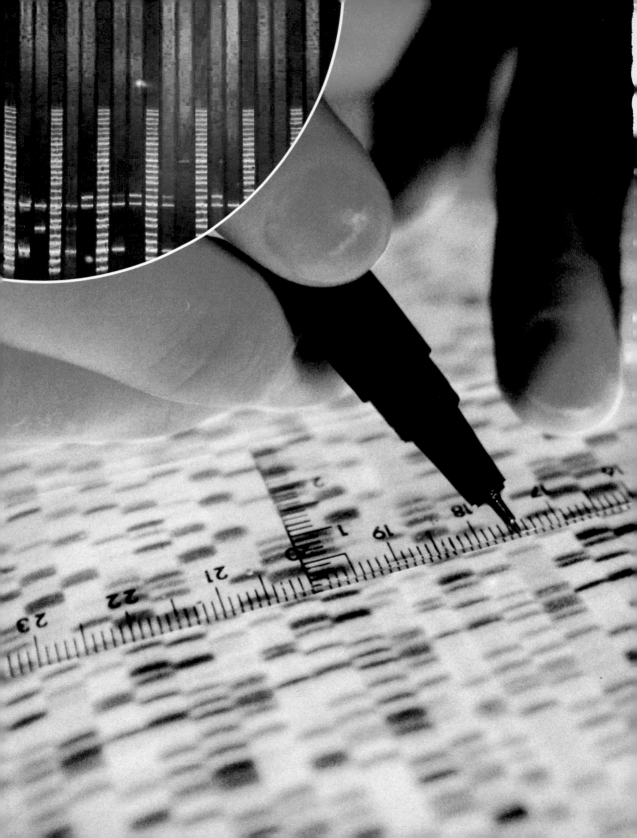

3

GENETIC FINGERPRINTS

A relative newcomer to forensic science, DNA has revolutionized the realm of the crime scene investigation. In recent years, DNA "fingerprinting" has received significant media attention for the criminal cases where it has been used either to exonerate the innocent or to exclude suspects. It also has a role to play in identifying the dead. The process has a number of advantages over other methods of identification, not least because every human being has a unique DNA profile, and his or her DNA makeup is identical in every single cell of the body. The tiniest trace of a suspect's blood, skin, saliva, or hair could be enough to convict.

CASE STUDIES:

- The Last of the Romanovs
- Free at Last
- Angel of Death
- DNA Fingerprints
- The Snowtown Monstrosities
- Murder at the "Piggy Palace"

What is DNA?

DNA, or deoxyribonucleic acid, is found in the center of almost all cells. It's packaged in 46 chromosomes that are stored inside a cell's nucleus. Under an electron microscope, DNA is an incredibly long and fine strand of material—around 6 feet (2 m) of it coils inside each cell.

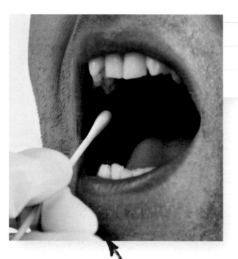

Cotton swabs are used for taking samples of cells from inside an individual's mouth. The swab is then sent to a laboratory, where the DNA is extracted from the cells and sequenced.

CELLULAR CODEWORK

DNA stores information—about cell formation, growth, and reproduction—and holds it in a form that cells find easy to duplicate. Both of these features make it valuable for forensic scientists. DNA is constructed using four different building blocks, which scientists call "bases."

The information is stored in a code created by the sequence of these bases. It is in effect a four-letter language, and the DNA inside each human cell consists of about three billion bases.

While much of our DNA is used to tell the body how to build and function itself, there are large stretches of "junk" DNA that don't appear to have any particular function. The length of these regions of junk DNA varies among different people, and forms a unique genetic fingerprint for each individual. But, just as a normal fingerprint doesn't give a picture of a person, a genetic fingerprint does not tell you anything about their genes. It is, however, a marker that can link evidence with a specific person. For example, in the case of the South Side Rapist (see page 91), police were able to place their prime suspect at the scene of three murders by matching the DNA from a sample of his hair to that of semen traces found at the crime scenes.

Running a DNA Test

1. A sample of human cells is needed to run a DNA test. Obvious examples include blood or body tissue found at a crime scene or semen collected from a rape victim. Using lab techniques to amplify a sample's amount of genetic material, scientists can work with minute quantities of material. A telephone receiver, an envelope's seal, or the rim of a used glass can contain enough cells for a scientist to examine.

2. DNA is extracted from a cell's nucleus using a salt solution, or a mixture of chloroform and phenol.

3. DNA is multiplied in a process called the polymerase chain reaction (PCR). A DNA molecule is like a spiraling ladder. The DNA is heated, splitting the "rungs" of the ladder and leaving two half-ladders. When the DNA cools, a new set of DNA building blocks will rebuild the missing sides of each half-ladder. Within a matter of minutes you have two new strands of DNA. Heat and cool again and you can go from two to four strands. A third cycle will create eight, and a fourth, sixteen. Each cycle takes as little as 20 minutes, so a scientist can quickly make copies of the original genetic data.

4. By a little bit of technical wizardry, scientists can manipulate this process so that they increase only the number of copies of the regions of DNA whose length varies between different people, and leave the rest basically untouched. Now the DNA just needs to be analyzed.

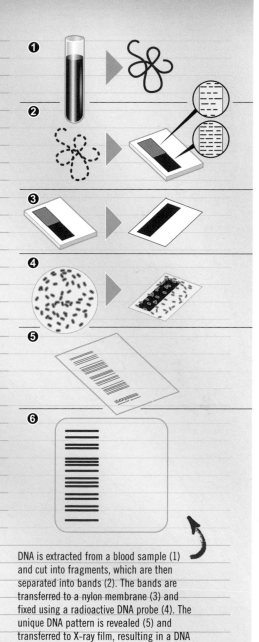

DNA is extracted from a blood sample (1) and cut into fragments, which are then separated into bands (2). The bands are transferred to a nylon membrane (3) and fixed using a radioactive DNA probe (4). The unique DNA pattern is revealed (5) and transferred to X-ray film, resulting in a DNA fingerprint (6).

The coded sequences in the arrangements of this DNA profile are unique to every individual. This is also known as a genetic fingerprint.

DNA Fingerprints

Scientists use a process called electrophoresis to separate the different variable regions and create a visual record of these. They place a sample of DNA in a small well cut into the surface of a gel spread over the top of a plate, and then apply an electrical current across the plate. DNA molecules naturally have a small negative charge on them, so the current can drag the fragments of DNA through the gel. The greater the charge on the DNA fragment, the faster it will travel, but smaller fragments meet less resistance and so travel faster than large ones. As each fragment of DNA will have a unique combination of charge, each will reach different places on the plate.

The result is a gel with a series of bars of DNA fragments in a line. Using a few chemicals allows scientists to see where the DNA is on the plate, and generate an image that looks a little like a badly constructed ladder. The spacing of the bars is unique for each individual, just as the pattern of whorls on his or her fingerprint is unique, and the image is known as a "genetic fingerprint."

DNA CONTROVERSY

Genetic fingerprints have become very controversial. Bio-statisticians argue about exactly how many variable regions need to be examined before we can be sure that no two people will share the same set. This is very important, because members of juries are easily swayed by an expert saying that a suspect's genetic fingerprint matches DNA found on a piece of evidence; this one piece of information can lead them to dismiss all other evidence and alibis. Also, just as a fingerprint is very different from a portrait, so too a DNA fingerprint says almost nothing about the person—it just happens that it's unique.

It may be that, in the future, DNA analysis will become so fast and cheap that investigators will be able to look at samples found at a crime scene and then search for specific information in the code-carrying region of the chromosomes that will show them the person's distinguishing features, such as hair color and stature. But for the moment that lies out of reach.

The ability of DNA analysis to come to conclusions based on minuscule samples is also a problem. Because a single hair is found at a site doesn't necessarily mean that the person was there. Just think how many hairs you must lose in a normal day at work or in public places. Imagine if one of these found its way to a crime scene, and you wound up charged with a crime, trying to explain that you weren't involved.

Evidence from DNA must be treated like all other evidence —it's useful, but it needs corroboration from other sources.

Who's the Daddy?

While DNA evidence has been a powerful tool to catch criminals, it has several additional uses. For example, it can identify the father of a child in a paternity dispute, because half of the genetic information in a child comes from the father. Analyzing the father and child will show if there are similarities in their DNA. If the child in question is a boy, then you can compare the Y chromosomes of both individuals, as this package of DNA only comes from the father. Investigators also use genetic fingerprinting to try to establish the identity of victims in situations where bodies have been rendered otherwise unidentifiable, as happened in Port Coquitlam, British Columbia, Canada (see page 80). Police investigating the disappearance of a number of prostitutes discovered numerous body parts on a local farm and used DNA fingerprinting as a means of identification.

And it is not just used on humans. DNA profiles can also be used to identify specific bacteria or viruses. This helped U.S. scientists pinpoint the source of the bacteria in the anthrax attacks that caused so much fear and disruption in 2001, though this information alone was not enough to track down the person who sent it.

The Innocent Go Free

Any useful forensic technique should be able to establish the truth, not simply gain a conviction. In other words, forensic science should be able to show that a suspect is innocent of the charges against him or her. Genetic fingerprinting is proving to be particularly good at doing this, and, thanks to DNA profiling, in recent years a number of convicts have had their cases repealed when genetic evidence showed that they had been wrongfully accused and convicted. For some, this has been a long time coming: in the case of David Milgaard (see page 73), some 27 years passed before his conviction was overturned on the basis of DNA fingerprinting.

DNA on File

One of the beauties of DNA fingerprinting is that information can be easily stored in a computer. Countries around the world are creating huge databases that record DNA from crime sites, convicted criminals, and—in some cases—members of the public.

- **The United States** The FBI's Combined DNA Index System (CODIS) has become an effective tool for solving violent crimes. CODIS enables federal, state, and local crime labs to exchange and compare DNA profiles electronically. Police can therefore use it to link crimes to each other, as well as to point them toward specific suspects. CODIS began as a small-scale project in 1990, but the DNA Identification Act of 1994 allowed the FBI to set up a national DNA law enforcement index. By 2003, all 50 states had laws requiring police to place DNA profiles of certain offenders on the CODIS database. By 2007, CODIS held just over five million profiles of convicts, as well as over 200,000 profiles of DNA found on physical evidence from numerous crime scenes.

- **Canada** Housed in the Royal Canadian Mounted Police Headquarters, in Ottawa, Canada's National DNA Data Bank has been in operation since July 2007, and is one of the most sophisticated tools of its kind. Investigating officers estimate that some 30,000 DNA samples are processed each year, each one taking just five days to analyze.

- **The United Kingdom** In the UK, the National DNA Database grows at about 400,000 profiles a year. This rapid increase is largely due to the policy of taking samples from anyone arrested for even the most minor offenses, and keeping them even if the person is not subsequently charged. The theory behind this policy is that most major crimes are committed by people who have also committed minor offenses. Civil liberties groups, however, are worried about this intrusion into people's lives, as well as being anxious about the misinterpretation of small fragments of DNA that may have arrived at a crime scene by chance. This rapid rate of sample collection meant that, at the beginning of 2006, there were over three million profiles recorded on the British database—five percent of the population (compared to 0.5 percent in the U.S. in CODIS). Police are excited by how these records can be used to solve cases. Authorities claim that in a typical month the DNA database points the finger of suspicion at individuals in 15 murder cases, 31 rapes, and 770 motor crimes.

- **Global** Created in 2002, Interpol's DNA database, the DNA Gateway, receives offender profiles from 46 member countries and currently has more than 73,000 profiles. The site is accessible across the globe, and is used primarily for the comparison of DNA data.

Jane Moira Taupin

Lead Scientist, LGC Forensics, Teddington, Middlesex, England

As a forensic biologist most of my examinations involve clothing items in the laboratory. I also attend crime scenes to examine blood patterns (BPA) and search for biological fluid. One of my specialties is the examination of damage to clothing.

Damage to the clothing of a victim, or indeed the perpetrator, is often found in crimes of violence such as homicide and rape, and may provide information as to the implement that caused the damage, the manner in which it was caused, and may corroborate or refute a particular crime scenario.

9:30 A.M. I receive a phone call from a detective regarding a crime scene I attended the previous weekend—the aggravated rape (with a knife) of an elderly woman in her home by an unknown male intruder. I had been asked to screen the carpeted floors of the kitchen and lounge for the presence of semen. I informed the detective that I could not confirm the presence of semen, nor could any DNA be obtained from the carpet samples I had removed. Furthermore, the medical samples from the victim showed no semen or foreign DNA. However, I informed the detective that there was a cut to the bra of the victim and that we had targeted this area for potential "touch" DNA from the offender. The detective replied that apparently the victim cut her clothing for ease of fit and the cut was not likely to be relevant to the case. I said that we had already sampled this area and results were due today.

10:30 A.M. I examine the jacket from a shooting scene in conjunction with laboratory notes from the other examiners. There was a large tear to the chest area of the jacket with bloodstains and some smaller holes around the periphery. There was also a spread of holes to the back of the shoulder and a smaller amount of bloodstains. The damage corresponded to shotgun pellet damage and indicated the shot to the chest was at a closer range than the shot to the shoulder. I sampled the bloodstain for DNA analysis and will later receive the results and compare with reference DNA profiles to determine whether the blood could be that of the specified victim.

1:00 P.M. I receive the DNA results from bra samples in a rape case and analyze them. There was a major/minor mixture of DNA; the major profile matched the victim. The minor profile matched a male individual and was suitable for a search on the national DNA database. I postulated the male DNA from the bra may have originated through contact with the offender over the period of hours that the victim was assaulted. I quickly received the results from the database search and they revealed that they matched only one person on the database in England. I rang the detective in the case and he said that the name I gave him matched one of four photographs he had on his desk of people with similar modus operandi. (The person was apprehended the following day having just pawned three rings that had belonged to the victim. He had just been released from prison five days prior to the rape. He later pleaded guilty to the rape).

CASE STUDY: The Last of the Romanovs

VICTIMS Russian Imperial family
CAUSE OF DEATH Gunshot wounds
WHERE Ekaterinburg, Russia
WHEN July 17, 1918

The Crime

After the Bolshevik Revolution, Nicholas II, the last tsar of Russia, and his family were moved under heavy guard to imprisonment at the Ipatiev House in Ekaterinburg in the Ural Mountains. Orders came from the Communist regime in Moscow that they were to be executed, and at 2:00 A.M. on July 17, 1918, they were lined up in the cellar of the house and shot, together with their physician, a maid, and two male servants. What happened to their bodies after that remained a mystery for decades.

The Case

Sixty years later, an Interior Ministry film producer named Gely Ryabov, made contact with the family of a guard, Yakov Yurovsky, who had seen the murders carried out. Ryabov discovered that the victims had initially been taken to a mineshaft called the Four Brothers, then moved along a long-abandoned cart track called the Koptyaki Road to a field north of the town where they were buried in boggy ground. With the help of local experts, Ryabov traced the route taken by the truck and on the burial site they found a layer of logs covering a pile of bones and fragments of quality clothing. The bones were stored in the Ekaterinburg morgue, and in 1991, Russian President Boris Yeltsin ordered an official inquiry to determine their identities.

The Evidence

Initial DNA analysis at the Home Office Forensic Science laboratories in the United Kingdom showed that five of the nine skeletons found were from the same family. Confirming the identity of that family, however, depended on establishing a link with surviving relatives through mitochondrial DNA, which is passed on through female relatives. Samples were collected by exhuming dead members of the family and by contacting living relations abroad. In all, the process of identification took seven years of painstaking testing, but at the end of January 1998, chief investigator Vladimir Solovyov announced that five skeletons were from the ruling family. Measurements of the bones established they were the Tsar and Tsarina, and their daughters Olga, Tatiana, and Anastasia. The remains of the heir to the throne, Alexei, and the Grand Duchess Maria were missing.

The Outcome

After the identification, President Yeltsin ordered that the remains should be interred in the Imperial family vault in the St. Peter and St. Paul Cathedral in St. Petersburg. On July 17, 1998, the 80th anniversary of the execution, the Tsar and his family were at last given a state funeral and reburial.

A portrait of the Russian Imperial family, 1913.

CASE STUDY: Free at Last

VICTIM Gail Miller
CAUSE OF DEATH Knife wounds
WHERE Saskatoon, Saskatchewan, Canada
WHEN January 31, 1969

Stony Mountain penitentiary in Winnipeg, Manitoba—David Milgaard's home for 20 years.

The Crime

On January 31, 1968, three young friends—David Milgaard, Ron Wilson, and Nichol John—were passing through Saskatoon on a trip across the Canadian prairies. As they stopped to pick up Albert Cadrain, a casual friend, 20-year-old nursing student Gail Miller failed to show up for her shift at the town hospital. Her partially naked body was found on a snowbank, and a postmortem showed that her throat had been cut, she had been stabbed 14 times, and there was evidence of rape.

The Case

When the police offered a reward for information, Cadrain claimed he had seen Milgaard return on the day of the murder with bloodstained clothing, and also that he was plotting to have witnesses murdered. Pressure was put on Wilson and John to change their original statements, which claimed that Milgaard had been with them at the time of the murder and could not have committed the crime. Despite his protestations of innocence, he was put on trial for the killing, was found guilty, and sentenced to life imprisonment on January 31, 1970.

The Evidence

For years Milgaard's family and defense team fought to have the case reopened, without success. In spite of the key prosecution witness, Albert Cadrain, having been admitted to a psychiatric hospital, the conviction stood. Only when samples of semen found on the victim's clothing were sent to a DNA laboratory in the United Kingdom did a report, issued on July 18, 1997, finally confirm that Milgaard was not connected to the murder. Furthermore, a check with Canadian criminal records revealed that the samples matched with a serial rapist named Larry Fisher, who had already served a total of 23 years in prison for rapes in Manitoba and Saskatchewan.

The Outcome

Fisher was arrested, charged with the murder, and sentenced to life imprisonment. Milgaard was given an official apology from the provincial government, and paid 10 million Canadian dollars ($8 million) in compensation for wrongful imprisonment. An official inquiry in September 2008 sharply criticized police for having ignored a tip in 1980 that Fisher had been the real killer. He had been given only cursory questioning because the entire focus of the investigation had targeted David Milgaard as a stranger in town at the time of the crime. Fortunately, in this case, DNA proved crucial in tracking down and identifying the guilty party, exonerating an innocent man.

CASE STUDY: Angel of Death

VICTIM Dr. Josef Mengele
CAUSE OF DEATH Drowning
WHERE Embu, Brazil
WHEN June 1985

as one bearing the name Wolfgang Gerhardt in the village of Embu in Brazil, where he had been buried at the age of 67 after a drowning accident in 1979. In June 1985, the grave was opened and a skeleton was removed for examination by a range of experts from the United States and Germany.

The Crime

Of all the horrors of the death camps operated by Hitler's Third Reich, few can equal the atrocities inflicted by "the Angel of Death," Dr. Josef Mengele. He carried out a series of sadistic experiments on his terrified victims, selected from among the inmates of the Auschwitz concentration camp. When the Nazi regime finally collapsed, Mengele fell into the Allies' hands, but amid the postwar chaos, he managed to escape to a new life in South America.

His family in Germany insisted he was dead, but there was a growing suspicion he may have survived, like so many other notorious missing Nazis, such as Deputy Führer Martin Bormann. Following the audacious Israeli capture of Adolf Eichmann, it was suggested that an official attempt be made to bring Mengele back to face justice too, but it was not until 1985 that the U.S. announced an investigation to track him down. This was likely to be a difficult task, as he would have spared no effort to invent a new identity in order to evade capture.

The Case

The task proved surprisingly easy: the evidence found the investigators rather than the other way around. A German couple named Wolfram and Lieselotte Bossert claimed they knew where the now-dead Mengele was buried, and identified his grave

The Evidence

Unfortunately, there was very little in the way of physical records relating to Mengele that could be used to verify the bones. His height was known to be 5 feet 8 inches (174 cm), and a dental chart from 1938 identified 12 fillings. The height of the skeleton, calculated from the bones of the leg and upper arm suggested a man around this height, and the dental chart showed a wider than usual space between two halves of the upper palate which accorded with his gap-toothed grin. Other tests were carried out: the shape of the pelvis suggested the skeleton was male, the shape of the nose and eye sockets suggested a Caucasian, and the amount of abrasion of the teeth suggested a subject who had been between 60 and 70 years old at death. But while all this evidence did not rule out the possibility the corpse was Mengele, it did not positively confirm it either.

German forensic anthropologist Richard Helmer, made a series of high-resolution video images of the skull, allowing photographs of Mengele to be superimposed on the appropriate image, so that individual features of the skull could be compared. The correlation between photos and video images was close enough for it to be highly probable that this was indeed the corpse of Josef Mengele.

The Outcome

Final confirmation had to wait until 1992, when DNA samples from Mengele's known living relatives in Germany were compared with samples produced from the skeleton exhumed from the grave. When the match was confirmed as positive, "the Angel of Death" was laid to rest at last.

The forensic team presents evidence identifying the exhumed skeleton as that of Dr. Mengele.

CASE STUDY: DNA Fingerprints

VICTIMS	Lynda Mann and Dawn Ashworth
CAUSE OF DEATH	Strangulation
WHERE	Narborough and Enderby, Leicestershire, United Kingdom
WHEN	September 1983 and July 1986

Dr. Alec Jeffreys, credited with the invention of DNA fingerprinting.

The Crime

In September 1983 and July 1986, two 15-year-old girls were raped and strangled in adjacent villages in the Leicestershire countryside. Both had been killed on secluded footpaths, so police assumed that both attacks were carried out by someone local, although the police did not at first connect the two incidents. The first victim, Lynda Mann, had been killed in Narborough, while the second, Dawn Ashworth, had been visiting friends in Narborough and was returning home to Enderby. Despite exhaustive inquiries in the area and appeals for witnesses, no positive leads emerged in either case.

The Case

After the second killing, police checked computer records for local men with records of sexual offenses. One positive lead pointed to Richard Buckland, a young kitchen porter at a mental hospital on the outskirts of Narborough, and when questioned, he admitted to Dawn Ashworth's killing. But when certain errors in the details of his story conflicted with the evidence, his confession was withdrawn. At this setback in the proceedings, police contacted Dr. Alec Jeffreys at the genetics department of Leicester University, who was famous for inventing DNA fingerprinting. They asked him to compare a sample of the suspect's DNA with evidence found on both the victims' bodies. The results were surprising. Buckland's sample matched neither of the others—but the samples from both victims were a perfect match, which meant the same person was responsible for both killings.

The Evidence

DNA analysis could now provide positive evidence of whether or not a suspect could be connected with the samples found at a crime scene, but this depended on investigators having DNA samples from the wider population to carry out comparisons. This meant requesting blood samples from the entire adult male population of Narborough and Enderby, as well as neighboring Littlethorpe as a first step. This was a huge task, involving more than 4,000 men between the ages of 16 and 34, and the cumbersome DNA comparison procedure then in use built up a large backlog. In any case, police knew the killer would try to avoid the test, but hoped that covering the entire male population in the area would eventually reveal who he was.

Then came a breakthrough that short-circuited their slow progress, and ended concerns over having to widen the search if a positive match was not identified. On August 1, 1987, four workers from a Leicester bakery were drinking in a Clarendon bar when one of them overheard a man named Ian Kelly admit he had been offered £200 ($285) by another fellow worker, Colin Pitchfork, to provide a blood sample on his behalf. The reason, according to Kelly, was that Pitchfork had once been convicted of indecent exposure, and police now gave him a rough time when under interrogation. Initially Kelly had refused, but Pitchfork explained that he had done the same thing for another friend with an indecent exposure conviction, and if he was found to have given two samples under different names in a murder investigation, he would be in really serious trouble. Kelly had agreed, and Pitchfork had provided him with a modified passport as proof of identity.

The Outcome

The woman who overheard this story knew Pitchfork as a persistent sexual pest, but was reluctant at first to incriminate him and Kelly. Finally, she told police seven weeks later, and they checked their records. Pitchfork had actually been questioned in the original door-to-door inquiries, but the genuine signature on his statement did not match the signature given by Kelly with the blood sample. Pitchfork was arrested and his blood sample showed he was indeed the double murderer. He later made a full confession, and on January 22, 1988, was sentenced to life imprisonment.

CASE STUDY: The Snowtown Monstrosities

VICTIMS 10 people
CAUSE OF DEATH Various causes
WHERE Snowtown, South Australia
WHEN 1993 to 1999

The Crime

Snowtown is a quiet little farming community some 90 miles (145 km) north of Adelaide in South Australia. Economic changes resulted in several businesses closing down, leaving derelict buildings in the town, one of which was the local branch of the State Bank of South Australia. On May 20, 1999, a police squad from Adelaide visited the town as part of the last stages of a major year-long operation, codenamed "Chart," which was searching for a group of three missing persons, one of whom had disappeared as early as 1993. They checked out the old bank building, and on opening the vault, their efforts were rewarded. They found six large 44-gallon (200-liter) plastic barrels, as well as an array of knives, handcuffs, ropes, rubber gloves, and a device for generating electric shocks. And when they checked the contents of the barrels, they found they were full of body parts and acid.

The Case

The three missing people—the initial reason for the search—were Clinton Douglas Tresize, missing since 1993; his friend Barry Wayne Lane, an alleged transvestite pedophile, missing since October 1997; and Elizabeth Haydon, a 37-year-old mother of eight, missing since earlier that year. Lane was alleged to have had a 10-year affair with a man named Robert Wagner, one of a group of three men that police

suspected of being involved in the disappearances, along with Mark Haydon, husband of the missing Elizabeth, and John Bunting.

Local people had noticed the group visiting Snowtown, and when police were checking on the empty buildings in the town, they were told that the bank vault had been rented to a man (later identified as one of the suspects) supposedly using it for storing kangaroo carcasses. All three suspects lived in the depressed northern suburbs of Adelaide, and were arrested on May 21, 1999. A fourth suspect, James Vlassakis, the 19-year-old son of Bunting's former girlfriend, was arrested two weeks later. When police searched Bunting's home they used ground-penetrating radar to find two more bodies, buried deep beneath the foundation of a rainwater tank.

The Evidence

When assembling the grisly evidence found in the old bank vault, investigators found they had fragments from eight different bodies, which, together with the ones dug up in Adelaide, made 10 total. Despite the effects of the acid, they managed to obtain fingerprints from some of the remains, but what also emerged from the investigation was a terrible tale of torture and mutilation. Some of the victims had been bound and gagged, some had feet and limbs brutally hacked off, and others had suffered burns and electric shocks.

The most unexpected breakthrough in the case was the degree to which the victims' DNA had survived in bones, hair, and body tissues. Samples of the victims' DNA were compared with that of relatives of the missing persons and, one by one, the victims were identified. An awful pattern was revealed: all the victims were known to the suspects

An aerial view of investigators digging in the backyard of a house in Snowtown, where the second body was found.

as friends or neighbors, and in some cases were actually related to them. They had been murdered for their relatively meager welfare payments, or to use their identities to take out bank loans. Some had been tortured into signing documents, or forced to record their voices on telephone answering machines to reassure family members who were worried about their disappearance.

The Outcome

When the quartet of suspects was brought to trial, Vlassakis admitted to murdering four of the victims, including his half-brother and stepbrother, and made an 800-page statement describing the role of the others. On September 9, 2003, the three others joined him in receiving life sentences after a trial that had lasted 11 months.

CASE STUDY: Murder at the "Piggy Palace"

VICTIMS	27 to 49 women
CAUSE OF DEATH	Various, including gunshot wounds and lethal injections
WHERE	Port Coquitlam, British Columbia, Canada
WHEN	1997 to 2002

The Crime

From the summer of 1983, prostitutes were regularly vanishing from Vancouver's red light district, the notorious downtown East Side. At the same time,

Robert "Willie" Pickton, a pig farmer from Port Coquitlam, hosted regular lurid gatherings featuring entertainment by Vancouver prostitutes at the "Piggy Palace," a nightclub building next door to his farm. Eventually, the missing-women investigation turned its attention to the Pickton farm, and on February 5, 2002, they arrived with a warrant to search for illegally held firearms. When they found an asthma inhaler belonging to one of the missing women, Pickton and his brother were arrested and a second warrant granted to search the entire property for traces of the missing women.

The Case

Searchers faced a colossal task. Because victims' bodies might have been cut up and fed to the pigs, special equipment, including diggers and powered conveyor belts, had to be used to find the smallest fragments of bone or tissue. They began with Pickton's own trailer and slaughterhouse, but it was only after two months of work that a freezer at the back of Pickton's property revealed the hands, feet,

MONA WILSON
NOVEMBER 2001

Steve Rix holds up a photo of his common-law wife, Mona Wilson, who went missing in the area in November 2001.

Dawn Crey, 41, who disappeared in 2000 and is believed to have died at the hands of Robert Pickton.

manure in an old pigpen, was traced to 32-year-old Brenda Wolfe, reported missing in April 2000. Bones from a left hand were identified as the remains of Georgina Papin, last seen in 1999. Another lower jaw fragment was that of Marnie Frey, missing since 1997. These remains were backed up by a mass of other material including hair, blood, semen stains, and small bone fragments amounting to more than 600,000 items found during the 20-month search. Skull damage suggested they had been split using a power saw, and all showed lethal gunshot wounds. Several items of clothing, jewelry, and papers with victims' DNA were also found around the property, including a jacket with traces of Wolfe's DNA inside Pickton's bedroom closet.

The Outcome

Pickton was put on trial on January 22, 2007, originally charged with murdering 27 women, whose remains had been found at the farm, but later reduced to the original six where evidence was most plentiful. His defense insisted that he had nothing to do with their deaths, and there was no DNA evidence of any direct contact with their body parts. Pickton also claimed that the skulls had not been split in the same way as he would split pig skulls when butchering them, but the prosecution insisted his experience as a butcher would have made it possible for him to have sawed them in half. On December 9, 2007, the jury found him not guilty of first-degree murder but guilty in all six cases of less premeditated second-degree murder. Four days later, he was sentenced to life imprisonment with no possibility of parole for 25 years.

and skulls of two of the missing women. Each skull had been sawed in half, but DNA confirmed the remains belonged to two of the missing women, 29-year-old Sereena Abotway and 22-year-old Andrea Joesbury, both of whom had disappeared in the summer of 2001.

The Evidence

The first gruesome finds at the Piggy Palace were merely the tip of the forensic iceberg. On June 4, 2002, two buckets found behind a slaughterhouse wall were found to hold the hands, feet, and bisected skull of 26-year-old Mona Wilson, who had disappeared seven months earlier. Two months later, a partial lower jawbone with a filled tooth, found in

4

BLOOD, SWEAT, AND TEARS

The examination and analysis of body fluids such as blood, saliva, semen, and urine—found on evidence collected from a crime scene or on the body of either victim or suspect—is called serology. The idea is that certain genetically inherited characteristics present in an individual's blood can also be found in some of these other physiological fluids, and can therefore be used to create a genetic profile of a potential suspect.

CASE STUDIES

- The South Side Rapist
- The Bloodstained Carpenter
- Dingo Attack?
- The Hypochondriac Killer
- Errors in Procedure

Does Red Equal Dead?

A large red stain or a red jellylike substance is found. While the first assumption is that this is a person's blood, there are three basic questions that need asking in sequence:

A casing lies in a pool of blood at the scene of a crime.

IS IT BLOOD?

Blood from all living creatures shares many basic similarities that enable a forensic expert to check a stain and quickly see if it's the work of an attacker or a prankster. The expert may drop a small piece of stained evidence in a solution and look for a color change. This method has been used since the turn of the twentieth century, and was crucial in the case of two boys who went missing in northern Germany in 1901 (see page 92).

Today's analysis relies on dropping a sample of the substance into a mix of the chemical compound, phenolphthalein, with hydrogen peroxide. If the solution rapidly turns pink, the sample contains blood. This occurs because blood contains peroxidase, an enzyme that rapidly breaks down hydrogen peroxide, and the phenolphthalein responds to this reaction.

One important thing about this test is that enzymes can operate at very low concentrations, so you need only a tiny amount of peroxidase in the sample to get a reaction. In other words, if done carefully this test will work on an item that has a remarkably small amount of blood.

Peroxidase is also used for detecting blood at a crime scene where, say, a violent death is thought to have occurred but no bloodstains can be seen (perhaps because the suspect cleaned the area before police arrived). Forensic scientists spray a special mixture of chemicals, called luminol, onto a large area and turn out the lights. The luminol causes a chemical reaction with the peroxidase, and glows wherever there is blood. The test is very sensitive. Even if bloodstains are diluted 300,000 times—a very thorough wash— luminol will still work. Luminol has another advantage: it doesn't damage the evidence. Once luminol has done its job, an expert can lift the trace of blood on a saline-soaked cotton swab and take it away for further analysis.

IS THE BLOOD HUMAN?

The body has a remarkable way of fighting infections that a forensic scientist can harness and put to use. When a foreign protein—such as a bacterium or virus—enters the body, it generates antibodies. These stick to the foreigners, and enable the body to destroy them. This sticking is highly specific. A particular type of antibody will only stick to one type of protein. Scientists have developed ways of building their own antibodies targeted at a huge range of substances that they are interested in finding. Some lock onto human blood, and can be used to confirm that a bloodstain did actually come from a human. Others lock onto blood from dogs, horses, sheep, or just about any animal you could think of. This means that scientists can say exactly what sort of living creature created the blood that left the stain.

These tests are not just limited to seeing what type of animal lost some of its blood, and they are not just limited to searching through a blood sample. One well-used antibody looks for THC-9-carboxylic acid, the chemical that turns up in a person's urine if they smoke marijuana. In this case, the antibody will still find trace evidence up to 10 days after a person has smoked the drug.

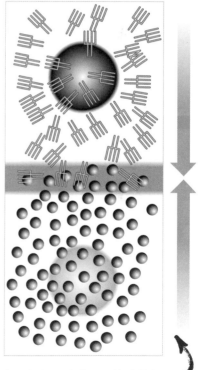

A precipitin test for human blood; if the substance is indeed human blood, a precipitin line forms where the antibodies meet the antigens as they diffuse along the gel plate.

WHOSE BLOOD IS IT?

Finding traces of blood at a crime scene is all well and good, but unless you can say from whom it came you are not much further forward. At the beginning of the twentieth century, Austrian scientist Karl Landsteiner discovered that blood can be classified into a number of distinct types. His work had an immediate impact on general medicine, as it explained that only certain blood types were compatible with certain others.

Later, determining a bloodstain's type became a routine part of forensic medicine. Although many people share the same blood type, police could nevertheless use blood analysis to narrow their hunt for a suspect considerably. For example, if blood left behind at the scene of a crime by a burglar was found to be type A, and one suspect's blood was type AB, then that suspect might be eliminated from the police investigation.

Over the decades, more and more features were found in the composition of blood that varied between individuals. Comparing a whole series of factors made blood analysis a much more powerful tool. Recent years have, however, seen blood types lose some of their importance, thanks to the significant scientific advances made by DNA analysis.

Telltale Signs

Blood spatters are often formed of blobs with a fine tail at one side. This pattern indicates that the blood was traveling fast when it hit the object and the tail points in the direction from which it came, meaning that experts can work out from exactly which direction the blood struck the object.

- If the stain is circular, blood struck the object straight on.
- If the stain is egg-shaped, blood came from an angle (the greater the angle, the more elongated the stain).

- If the blood traveled at great speed, say, propelled by a bullet, the droplet will be surrounded by myriad smaller flecks.
- A smeared bloodstain indicates that someone rubbed against it. That person will be carrying a stain, probably on a trouser leg or their coat.

BLOOD-SPATTER PATTERNS

Blood can tell you more than simply whose veins it used to flow through. The pattern of the stain can determine where a person was when the blood escaped, and whether he or she was alive or dead at the time. A large pool of blood shows that the person was alive in that spot for some time after receiving a wound; dead bodies stop bleeding quickly when the heart stops pumping blood around the body.

If spatter marks are very clear, you can learn a great deal about the weapon used. When someone stabs or beats a person to death, the killer does not swing the weapon in a straight line, but rather in a curve, and the direction of the curve in the spatter shows whether the weapon had been held in the left or right hand.

Quite often, both the victim and assailant will lose blood at a crime scene, so it's important to determine whose blood makes up each separate mark.

A spatter is made by blood dropping from a height. The spatter forms as circular drips, because the blood is hitting the surface straight on.

A narrow track of blood suggests that something fine, such as a sharp knife, was used, while a broad band of blood spatters could suggest something more like a baseball bat. These marks also give clues about how frenzied the attack was, and how many blows the killer gave. Finally, an area of floor with no blood can be just as revealing as the rest of a blood-spattered scene. Obviously something had stood there during the attack. It may be that the shape of that clear space could match an important box, bag, or container that has been taken away.

Sexual Assault

Collecting evidence in a situation where a person claims to have been raped or sexually assaulted is a particularly sensitive issue, because the victim has just been through a traumatic and highly personal ordeal. Then specially trained investigators called sexual assault nurses (forensic nurses) ask the person to go through an invasive examination so that they can recover any evidence that may be left behind. Accusing someone of rape is a serious charge, so courts demand a high level of evidence before they will convict.

The fingernail from a rape victim—with forensic evidence in the form of blood, skin, and semen from the aggressor—can be used for DNA analysis to identify the assailant.

SUSPICIOUS SUBSTANCES

Owing to the physical violence that is part of a sexual assault, there's a chance that blood will have transferred from the attacker to the victim. Traces of semen are also often found on the victim or clothing. Consequently, swab samples are taken from any region of the body where the victim claims that sexual contact occurred. And if the victim says the attacker bit, kissed, or licked anywhere, then that part of the body is swabbed particularly carefully, because DNA techniques could well recover a genetic fingerprint. Experts also need a seven milliliter sample of the victim's blood to rule out any blood smears that may have come from her.

On top of this, there's every chance that a forensic specialist could find some of the attacker's hair, or fibers from the attacker's clothing clinging to the victim. Scraping under the victim's fingernails can also be particularly productive, as there could easily be a mass of the attacker's cells embedded there if the victim fought back during the assault. Finally, the forensic investigator collects a sample of the

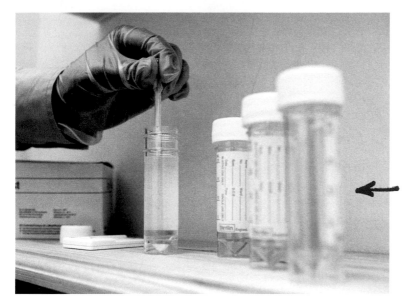

Tests on a victim's urine sample could indicate that a "date rape" drug was administered by the assailant.

victim's urine so that the forensic laboratory can look for evidence of a "date rape" drug.

SPERM COUNT

It may be that the person accused has been detained, in which case investigators will be very keen to examine his clothing for reciprocating evidence. The most valuable item will probably be the suspect's underwear. If a penetrative sexual attack has occurred, there's a good chance that DNA techniques will be able to find traces of the victim's DNA.

Locating a patch of semen can often be a matter of searching for a suspicious dry, crusty mark. But looking for small spots can be harder. Now, forensic experts have to introduce a bit of science. Semen does not just contain sperm, but is also loaded with biological molecules that help sperm make it to the egg. One of these molecules, acid phosphatase, can be detected using what's known as the acid phosphate test. A forensic technician lightly rubs a moistened piece of filter paper over the suspected area, picking up any traces of semen on the paper. Then a drop of acidic sodium naphthylphosphate and Fast Blue B dye is placed on the paper. If the paper picked up some acid phosphatase, the dye will turn purple—a positive result. Now microscopic analysis may be used to locate sperm, or DNA techniques used to collect genetic material. Either way, confirming the presence of semen will strengthen the prosecution's case.

Marty Coyne

Chief Forensic Photographer, Allegheny County Coroner's Office, Pennsylvania, United States

As chief forensic photographer, I am called to all major crime scenes in the district, where I make photographic recordings of the undisturbed scene, which may then be used as evidence in the case. I need to be available 24 hours a day, seven days a week.

4:00 A.M. The telephone jangles me awake and gets me out of bed. It is the emergency dispatcher, telling me that I am needed at a death scene; a body has been found in a vehicle parked near the river. The outside temperature is in the single digits, so warm clothes are essential; I could be outside for several hours.

4:45 A.M. When I arrive, the detectives are already there. The passenger-side window has been shattered, and the individual in the driver's seat has what appears to be a gunshot wound to the head. I start taking photographs, on my own initiative and at the request of the scene investigators. First, I document the outside of the vehicle, then the shattered window and the glass fragments inside, followed by the victim seated in the vehicle. I take care not to miss the small things, such as anything in or near the hands and whether the feet are on any of the pedals. I pay particular attention to the wound, and any blood trails and drops on the body.

7:00 A.M. Once the body has been removed, I take a full-face ID photograph, along with photos of anything on the body or clothing that may be of value or interest.

7:45 A.M. Once again, attention is turned to the vehicle and surroundings. The positions of the transmission lever and the ignition key are documented, as are any items on the seats. If there are any shoe impressions nearby, they will be

photographed, as well as the contents of trash cans and possibly even an adjacent drain. In some instances, more images may be needed of the vehicle when it is examined at the forensic lab.

9:15 A.M. Now it is time to head for the coroner's office to document the autopsy being performed on the victim. The body, dressed just as it was when removed from the vehicle, is placed on the autopsy table, and overall views are taken.

9:45 A.M. The forensic pathologist and autopsy technicians go over the corpse, describing the body and clothing. Findings that may become important are photographed as they come to light.

10:45 A.M. The body is undressed and the process repeated. After the body has been washed, photos are taken of any injuries, along with the damage caused by the gunshot. The hands are photographed to show the presence or absence of defense wounds. Damage to any organ is photographed, usually "as found" and again on a special stand.

11:45 A.M. Items such as bullets are also recorded "in situ," or in their natural position, and on the photo-stand.

12:30 P.M. The exposed film goes to our own photo lab; it is essential that we keep custody of this valuable evidence. Occasionally, I am called to court to testify to that fact.

CASE STUDY: The South Side Rapist

VICTIMS Debbie Dudley Davis, Dr. Susan Hellems, Diane Cho, and Susan Tucker

CAUSE OF DEATH Strangulation

WHERE Richmond, Virginia, United States

WHEN 1987

The Crime

In late 1987, four women were violently raped and strangled in Richmond, Virginia. The four victims—Debbie Dudley Davis, Dr. Susan Hellems, Diane Cho, and Susan Tucker—were of similar appearance; all had been attacked while asleep; all had been bound and gagged using ropes and duct tape; all had been violently raped; and all had been strangled.

The Case

The strong similarities in the way all four crimes had been committed led police to believe they were the work of one man. Further notable aspects of the crimes were that the killer had been skilled at gaining access to the homes of his victims and clearly had not been fazed by the presence of other members of a victim's family in nearby rooms. Hairs recovered from the scenes indicated that he was an African-American.

The police thought it was likely that he was an experienced burglar. It appeared that the "South Side Rapist," as he had been dubbed by the media, had selected his victims carefully and police sought a link between them to indicate why they had been chosen. Eventually, they realized that all four women had visited a particular shopping mall, and it was likely that this was the murderer's hunting ground.

The Evidence

The Virginia Police mounted a surveillance operation at the shopping mall and noticed that a known local cat burglar, Timothy Spencer, spent a considerable amount of time loitering there. When he was pulled in for questioning on an unrelated burglary charge, police used the opportunity to take blood, saliva, and hair samples from him, for the recently introduced technique of DNA profiling. Forensic scientists were astounded when the samples provided a genetic match with traces of semen found at the scenes of three of the murders—those of Tucker, Davis, and Hellems. The odds of finding another match were considered to be as high as 135 million to one: they had their killer.

The Outcome

Timothy Spencer was sent to trial for the murder of the fourth victim, Susan Tucker. The DNA evidence formed a major part of the prosecution case, and Spencer was convicted.

Subsequently, the combination of the crimes' "signature" and the DNA evidence left the jury in no doubt that he had carried out the other killings. It also suggested that he had been responsible for two additional murders—one of which had happened three years earlier, in 1984, and which now resulted in the freeing of someone who had been wrongfully convicted for it.

On April 28, 1994, Timothy Spencer was the first man in the United States to be executed largely on the basis of DNA "fingerprinting."

CASE STUDY: The Bloodstained Carpenter

VICTIMS Hermann and
Peter Stubbe

CAUSE OF DEATH Blows to the head

WHERE Gohren, Rugen, Germany

WHEN July 1, 1901

The Crime

Today's forensic scientists have a formidable battery of tests and techniques to unravel the secrets at a crime scene. Yet just over a century ago, it was impossible to even determine whether apparent bloodstains really were human blood. In the case of the death of two young German brothers, eight-year-old Hermann and six-year-old Peter Stubbe, catching their killer depended on the first use of a reliable test. On the afternoon of July 1, 1901, the brothers had failed to return to the family home in the village of Gohren on the island of Rugen on the Baltic coast of northern Germany.

The next day, searchers found their dismembered bodies scattered in nearby woods. The skulls were smashed, Hermann's heart was missing, and a jagged and bloodstained stone found nearby was almost certainly the murder weapon. There was even a potential suspect: a fruit seller had seen a local carpenter talking to the boys on the afternoon they vanished. He was an oddly behaved, reclusive man named Ludwig Tessnow, who lived in the nearby village of Baabe. Police searched his home and workshop, and found clothes and boots bearing dark stains, although the clothes had been thoroughly washed. Tessnow explained that the marks were simply wood dye used in his work and the police, unable to prove otherwise, had no grounds for charging him.

The Case

Under the German legal system, cases were first pursued by the local examining magistrate, in this case a man named Johann Schmidt. He recalled a strikingly similar case on September 8, 1898, in the village of Lechtingen, near Osnabruck, where two young girls had vanished. The next day their bodies had been found hacked to pieces, and local police had hunted for possible suspects. Their search turned up a carpenter named Ludwig Tessnow, who had been brought in for questioning as his clothing was heavily stained. On that occasion, too, he had claimed the stains were wood dye used in his work, and as a result he had been released and never charged. There was even a third case, involving animals rather than children. On June 11, 1901—less than a month before the disappearance of the two brothers—a local farmer had found seven sheep disemboweled and hacked to pieces, and had seen a man running away from the scene at his approach. At a police line-up, he picked out Ludwig Tessnow as the man he had seen.

The Evidence

It was clear to Schmidt, and to prosecutor Ernst Hubschmann, that the only way to prove Tessnow was the killer was to disprove his claim that the stains on his clothing were wood dye. Then Schmidt learned that a biologist at Griefswald University, Professor Paul Uhlenhuth, had developed a reliable test for identifying bloodstains, which could even distinguish between human and animal blood, using serums from different animals to make the identifications. Items of Tessnow's clothing were confiscated and sent to the university laboratories for testing. The complex procedure took several days,

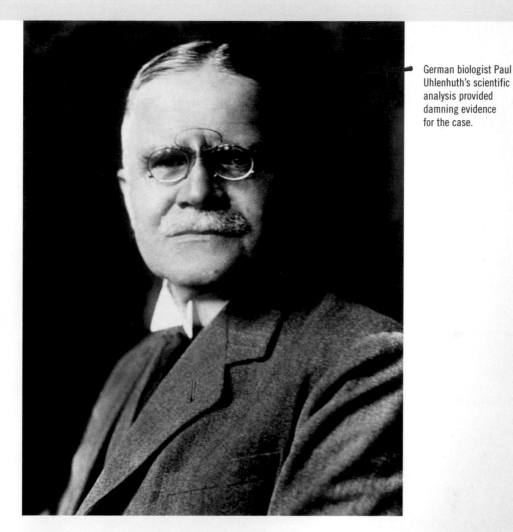

German biologist Paul Uhlenhuth's scientific analysis provided damning evidence for the case.

but at the end the evidence was clear. On August 8, 1901, Uhlenhuth reported that he had tested more than 100 dark spots showing on the clothing. He found there were indeed spots of wood dye on the overalls, and patches of sheep's blood on the jacket, but there were 17 distinct spots of human blood on his suit, shirt, overalls, and hat.

The Outcome

This proof that Tessnow's clothing was indeed stained with the blood of his victims was exactly what the prosecutors needed. He was put on trial for the murder of the young brothers, found guilty, and executed in Griefswald Prison in 1904, only a short distance from the laboratory that had developed the tests that proved his guilt.

CASE STUDY: Dingo Attack?

VICTIM Azaria Chamberlain
CAUSE OF DEATH Animal attack
WHERE Ayers Rock, Northern Territory, Australia
WHEN August 17, 1980

The Crime

In August 1980 Michael and Lindy Chamberlain took their two young sons, Aidan and Reagan, and their baby daughter, Azaria, on a camping holiday in Australia's remote interior. They set up their tent at a tourist site close to Ayers Rock, known to Aboriginals as Uluru. On the evening of August 17, Azaria was asleep at the back of the tent with Reagan. Aidan was with his mother at the campsite grill where she was cooking supper, just 20 yards (18 m) from their tent. At around 8:00 P.M., Michael heard a cry and Lindy rushed back to the tent. She saw a dingo emerge from the tent with something in its mouth, which it was shaking furiously. She looked for the baby, but she was gone. The alarm was raised, search parties were sent out, but Azaria was never seen again.

The Case

On August 25, a tourist discovered some baby clothes, apparently neatly arranged, to the west of the rock. They were Azaria's, and showed traces of blood, though the jacket was missing. The clothes were checked for traces of dingo hair or saliva, but none were found. Reports indicated there were no tears in the clothing to suggest dingo bites, and investigators suggested the baby had been abducted and attacked, and her clothes left far from where she had been snatched.

A picture of the baby, Azaria Chamberlain, taken not long before the dingo attack in August 1980.

To back this up, they cited mistakes in the way the baby's clothes had been fastened and the presence of small adult handprints in the bloodstains. This leveled suspicion at the parents. Their automobile was searched and traces of blood spray were found on the carpet, around the seat supports, and on a pair of scissors in the vehicle. The Chamberlains were tried for the murder of their daughter in September 1982, and both were convicted.

The Evidence

The verdict caused a furious reaction in Australia. Apart from sympathy for the parents, there were criticisms about restrictions placed on the defense and the standard of the evidence. For example the "blood spray" found in the automobile was later identified as a General Motors sound-deadening material, Dufix HN1081, sprayed under the vehicle during manufacture, and which entered the interior through a hole in the wheel arch. The same pattern was found on other examples of that model, and in all cases showed positive in the tests for blood. Another test showed infant hemoglobin in the

The vacation to Ayers Rock, a tourist destination for so many travelers to Australia, turned into this family's worst nightmare.

vehicle, but the Chamberlains lived in Mount Isa, which was a copper-mining district, and most everyday objects picked up microscopic copper deposits, which showed positive in the hemoglobin test. Finally, the damage to the baby's clothes was found to show ample evidence of bites, tears, and even dingo hairs, but this was only checked two years after the trial.

The Outcome

Two appeals were rejected in spite of these conflicts. Only when Azaria's missing jacket was found more than five years later in a dingo's cave near the campsite, spattered with blood and badly torn, was Lindy's conviction reversed. She was released on February 7, 1986, and both she and Michael were finally cleared in September 1988. Since then there have been several dingo attacks on children of different ages, at least one of them fatal.

CASE STUDY: The Hypochondriac Killer

VICTIMS The Laitner family
CAUSE OF DEATH Knife wounds
WHERE Dore, Sheffield, England
WHEN October 23, 1983

The Crime

On October 23, 1983, the Laitner family was celebrating the marriage of their daughter in a rented tent at their house in the Sheffield suburb of Dore. A dangerous criminal was watching the event from the cover of some nearby bushes—his interest, Nicole Laitner, the 18-year-old sister of the bride.

Eventually the celebration ended. The house was in darkness when the intruder broke in through a patio door, and killed both Nicole's parents and her brother in a series of knife attacks. He seized the terrified girl, dragged her out to the wedding tent, and then violently raped her. He then forced her back into her bedroom and raped her twice more, before tying her up and vanishing into the night. She escaped by first light and the search for the killer began.

The Case

The inside of the house was awash with blood. Most was clearly from the three murder victims, yet there were apparent exceptions. There was blood on the girl's nightgown and on her bed approximately at knee level, but she herself had not lost any blood. It seemed this blood might have come from the attacker, who must have injured himself somehow. Samples were sent to the Home Office Forensic Science Service at Wetherby for analysis, where a series of different factors—type, rhesus factor, and the presence of specific proteins—identified a rare combination, present in only 0.002 percent of the population, and this particular combination had already appeared in police records. A month before the Laitner killings, a woman had been raped in Selby. The suspect was a violent criminal named Arthur Hutchinson. Unfortunately, he had escaped from custody on September 28 by jumping through a window and scrambling across a high wall topped with barbed wire. It was this that had cut his leg badly, and it seemed likely that this wound had opened up again when he attacked Nicole.

The Evidence

Hutchinson was a known hypochondriac, visiting ER departments on the slightest pretext. A statement was issued that the barbed wire on top of the wall where he had escaped from custody had been given special treatment, and anyone who had come into close contact with it should seek medical attention, in case gangrene set in. He turned up at the Royal Infirmary in Doncaster, where he was treated for a gash to his knee, and police were able to arrest their prime suspect. Not only did Nicole positively identify him as her attacker, but his shoes were matched to a footprint in the blood on the stairs at her family's house, and he had left a clear handprint on a bottle of champagne in the tent.

The Outcome

Hutchinson was put on trial on September 4, 1984, and his defense collapsed after the prosecution introduced the watertight forensic evidence. After a 10-day trial, he was found guilty of the rape and murders, and was jailed for life.

CASE STUDY: Errors in Procedure

VICTIMS Nicole Brown-Simpson
and Ronald Goldman

CAUSE OF DEATH Throat wounds

WHERE Los Angeles, California,
United States

WHEN June 12, 1994

The Crime

O.J. Simpson was world famous as both a football star and a film actor. In 1985, he married Nicole Brown-Simpson and the couple had two children. Cracks in the relationship began to appear, and eventually Simpson's violent behavior led to divorce, in 1992. Then, on the misty Sunday evening of June 12, 1994, neighbors living close to Nicole's home in the Los Angeles suburb of Brentwood were disturbed by the agitated barking of her dog. When they tried to calm it down, they saw its paws were soaked in blood. Approaching the house they could clearly see a body lying inside the gate, and immediately called police to the scene.

The Case

The body was that of Nicole, and close by was the body of her friend Ronald Goldman. Both had bled to death after horrific throat wounds. Police tried to contact Simpson, who lived five minutes' drive away, but he had left earlier that evening on a trip to Chicago. On his return he was at first questioned informally by the police, but as more and more evidence started to point to him as the killer, police issued an arrest warrant on June 17. Simpson and his lawyer failed to report as ordered, but Simpson was spotted driving his Ford Bronco, accompanied by close friend Al Cowling, who warned police that their suspect was suicidal. A bizarre chase ensued, shown on television, with police pursuing the runaway vehicle at 40 miles per hour (65 kmph), followed by helicopters, until the fugitive finally drove back to his home and submitted to arrest.

The Evidence

On the face of it, the evidence against Simpson was damning. Numerous people had heard him threaten his ex-wife, and he had broken into her previous home and attacked her. DNA profiling of the blood at the crime scene showed the presence of a third person's blood, later matched to that of Simpson. At his initial interview, police noticed that his left hand was cut—a bloody left-hand glove was found beside the bodies, the right-hand glove was outside Simpson's home. Drops of the victims' blood were found in Simpson's Ford Bronco, and at his home.

The Outcome

It was difficult to find a more watertight mass of evidence, yet in the end Simpson was acquitted. His energetic 11-lawyer defense team attacked every conclusion of the forensic team, and insisted the actions of the investigators were governed by racism and personal malice. For example, Simpson said he had never owned a pair of Bruno Magli shoes, matched to shoe prints at the scene, even though press photographs clearly showed him wearing them. When he was asked to try on the gloves in court, his lawyer insisted he try them on over a pair of latex gloves, so unsurprisingly they were too small.

The trial lasted for nine months, but in the end the jury was divided and the crime remains unsolved, a powerful example to underline that even first-class forensic evidence can be rendered useless by small errors in collecting samples and procedures.

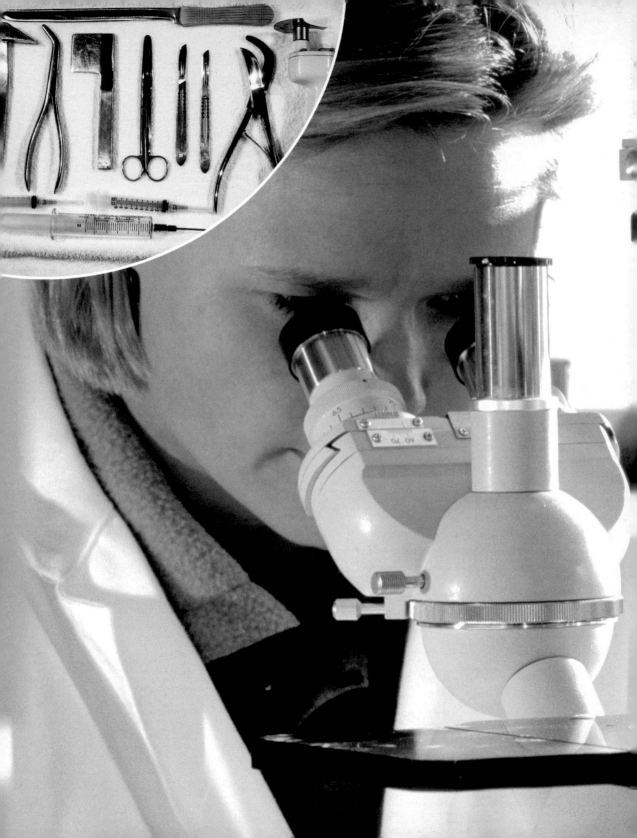

5

WHAT'S YOUR POISON?

Following the autopsy of a suspicious death, a forensic toxicologist will be asked to examine various body fluids of the deceased to help determine how he or she died. Using an arsenal of analytical methods and specialized equipment, the scientist analyzes blood, urine, and bile samples as well as sections of organs, such as the liver or brain. In many cases, the aim is to detect whether a poison or drug overdose might have contributed to the person's death, and to determine how it might have been administered —either voluntarily or by force.

CASE STUDIES:
- The Fugitives
- A Dose of Death
- A Deadly Cup of Tea
- Accidental Poisoning?
- Killer Painkillers
- A Deadly Umbrella Attack
- 'Till Death Do Us Part
- A Fatal Bedside Manner
- The Polonium Trail

Chemical Killers

Toxic chemicals and drugs span a massive range, from alcohol, which is seen as a socially acceptable drug, to those such as heroin and crack cocaine, which are universally frowned upon. Toxic chemicals also include lethal substances like arsenic and ricin, which can be used as tools of aggression, or for suicide.

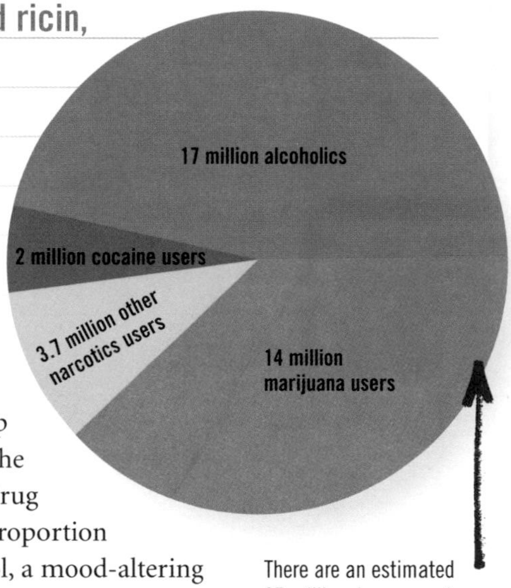

17 million alcoholics

2 million cocaine users

3.7 million other narcotics users

14 million marijuana users

WHO'S USING WHAT?
Estimates suggest that up to 37 million people in the United States are illicit drug users, with the highest proportion being addicted to alcohol, a mood-altering drug that's illegal in situations where consumption could be dangerous.

There are an estimated 37 million drug users in the United States. The chart above illustrates the proportion addicted to each drug type.

Up to 75 percent of the work in a forensic science laboratory may be related to drugs.

Selling illegal drugs like heroin and cocaine is big business, and vast fortunes have been made by those involved in the trade. The amount of money at stake encourages people to go to extreme lengths, including violence, to protect their interests. For evidence gatherers at drug-related crime scenes, there's the obvious task of looking for stashes of tablets, powders, or blocks of resin, as well as searching for the signs of drug use such as needles and syringes, or in some cases

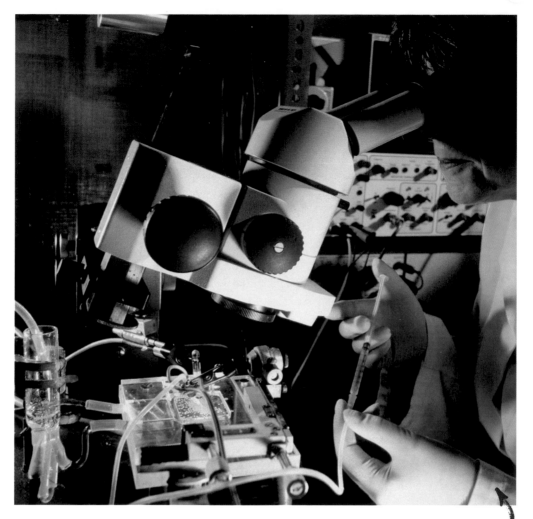

the paraphernalia of drug manufacturing. But evidence isn't just left lying around. Often the more important evidence is a part of the victim or suspect.

When someone inhales, ingests, or injects a drug, it moves into his or her bloodstream and circulates around the body. Therefore, taking and analyzing a blood sample can be one way of capturing evidence of use. To have a good chance of tracking down drugs, a forensic specialist needs about 10 milliliters of blood, though some of the newer test procedures can now work on smaller samples. Urine is also a good sample to use for examination and analysis, as the body sends many of the chemicals it would rather not have floating around to the bladder.

A toxicologist uses a microscope to examine traces of chemicals in some muscle tissue.

One of the problems faced by any toxicologist is that drugs don't just enter the body, perform their action, and then leave in the person's urine. The body's biochemical machinery normally alters a drug's molecules while it remains in the body. This means that a toxicologist spends most of her time looking for chemical byproducts that indicate that a drug has been used, rather than searching for the drug itself.

GROWING CRYSTALS

In order to identify the chemicals contained in a powder, experts simply dissolve a small quantity of the sample in a drip of carefully selected liquid placed on a microscope slide—and wait. In a few hours, the drug starts to appear in the form of crystals, which have a highly characteristic shape. One such procedure was developed as early as the 1820s, by London chemist, James Marsh, and was used to detect traces of arsenic in the bodies of the victims of Dr. Arthur Warren Waite (see page 108).

The problem with most forensic drug evidence is that the sample is not always pure. The active drug is likely to be either not particularly highly refined or deliberately mixed with some diluting agent. To get around this, a forensic laboratory often performs some form of chromatography on it, and compares the results with reference samples that they have carried out with known ingredients. The ultimate test is probably to combine gas chromatography with mass spectrometry.

The process of chromatography separates the sample into individual ingredients, and the mass spectrometer smashes these into little pieces and analyzes what comes out, giving a reading that is highly specific for each individual compound.

Toxicology

Toxicology—the study of poisons and their effects—plays a part in forensics at three levels:

• A criminalist may be asked to see if a person's behavior has been influenced by a drug.

• A forensic team may examine evidence to see whether a suspect has been manufacturing illicit compounds.

• Forensic experts will look for evidence that a toxic substance has killed a person.

Drug Indicators

Some of the simplest screening tests look for a specific color change when part of the evidence is placed in a known solution:

- Drop **heroin** or **morphine** in a mixture of formaldehyde and sulfuric acid and the liquid turns purple.
- The same solution turns orange-brown with **amphetamines**.
- Add some dilute cobalt acetate to some methanol and pour this over the sample before topping up with a little isopropylaine mixed with methanol, and the solution will turn violet-blue if a **barbiturate** was present.
- **LSD** can be detected by a solution, containing the chemical p-dimethylaminobenzaldehyde in hydrochloric acid and ethyl alcohol, turning blue-purple. The test is often difficult to perform at a crime scene, because **LSD** is used in such small quantities.
- A three-stage test can show whether a powder contains **cocaine**. Add the powder to cobalt thiocyanate dissolved in water and glycerin, and the solution turns blue. Pour in some hydrochloric acid and it now turns pink. Finally, add chloroform; if the solution turns blue in the chloroform layer, the sample contains cocaine.

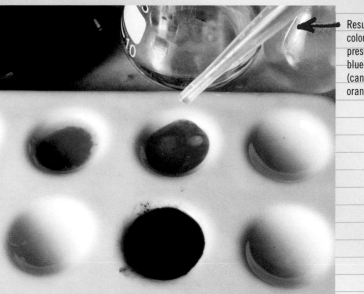

Results of drug tests, colors indicating the presence of a drug: blue (cocaine), black (cannabis), and orange (amphetamine).

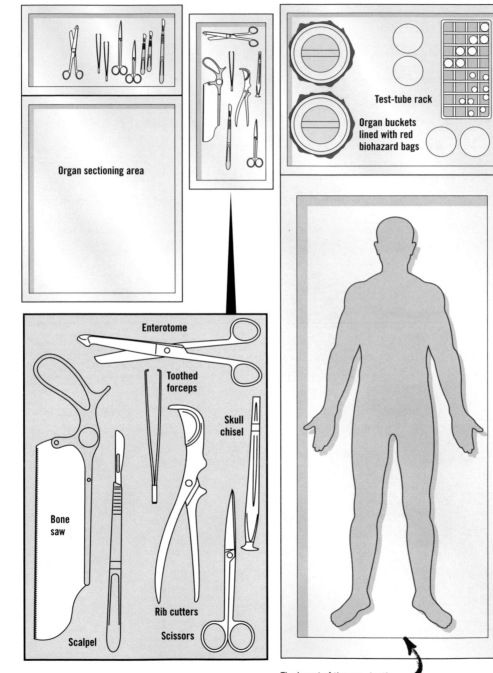

Organ sectioning area

Test-tube rack

Organ buckets
lined with red
biohazard bags

Enterotome

Toothed
forceps

Skull
chisel

Bone
saw

Rib cutters

Scalpel

Scissors

The layout of the examination
area in the autopsy suite.

SPOTTING KILLER CHEMICALS

When death by poisoning is suspected, investigators can be much more invasive than is possible with living victims. A pathologist who works on criminal cases (a forensic pathologist) performs an autopsy and passes over a sizable mass of tissue and other samples to the lab. These samples may include the entire stomach contents, half the person's liver, both kidneys, all the urine from the bladder, and half the brain. The pathologist also collects blood from the right and left chambers of the heart, as well as from other sites around the victim's body. On top of this, the spleen is sent for testing if there is any suspicion that cyanide was involved, because cyanide particularly affects this organ.

In some cases, it is possible for a forensic lab to work on an almost entirely decomposed body, as some poisons, such as arsenic, can be detected for an extended period of time in hair, nails, and bone—body parts that survive decomposition. Other chemicals leave traces for years, such as the thallium that killed Caroline Grills's victims (see page 110), or the morphine overdoses administered by Dr. Harold Shipman (see page 117). In both cases, it was an examination of exhumed bodies that led to their conviction.

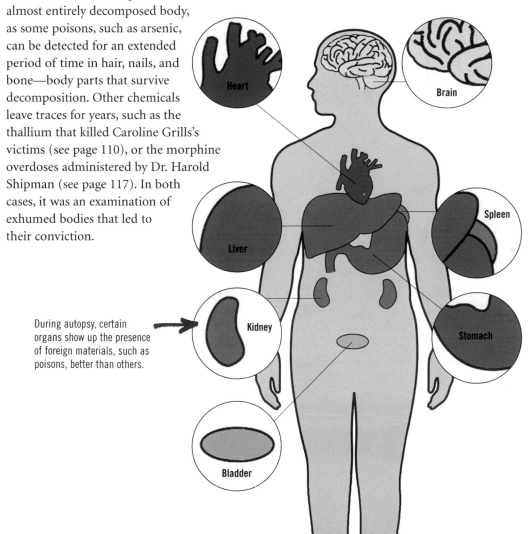

During autopsy, certain organs show up the presence of foreign materials, such as poisons, better than others.

Heart

Brain

Spleen

Liver

Stomach

Kidney

Bladder

Dr. Frederick W. Fochtman

Chief Toxicologist, Allegheny County Coroner's Office, Pennsylvania, United States

forensic toxicologist

As a forensic toxicologist, each day I find myself looking at a variety of blood, body fluids, and organ tissues submitted from recent deaths of undetermined origin. Opening the containers cautiously, I remove portions to test.

9:30 A.M. Having checked any overnight telephone and email messages, I begin to prepare samples for analysis using a variety of instruments, such as immunoassay analyzers, gas and liquid chromatographs, gas chromatography/mass spectrometers, gamma counters, and head-space analyzers. Once these instruments produce all their data, I have to interpret the information and come up with answers regarding the cause of death.

11:00 A.M. Local police officers have asked me to evaluate specimens and cases for an incident that happened earlier this morning, when a worker who suffered a minor automobile accident was subjected to a routine drug screening by his company.

> "In some cases, it can be immediately apparent that the person has been dead for some time."

12 NOON Tests run on his urine sample, reveal that it proves positive for morphine. Looking at the case notes, I learn that the driver claims to have eaten almost all of a box of crackers before reporting for work this morning. The crackers in question had poppy seeds baked into them, and poppies are the source of morphine, so I set about arranging an experiment that will help me evaluate and interpret the data further.

1:15 P.M. Specimens have just been submitted from a case that is suspected to be a lethal overdose of a prescription drug that has been approved recently by the FDA and is being given frequently to patients with chronic pain. There have been reports of misuse of the drug and possible overdoses.

1:45 P.M. I start to assess the evidence by searching literature for information about analytical methods and case reports. I also order a sample of the drug to use as a standard. When this arrives, I intend to prepare various reagents to properly validate the assessment. Upon analyzing the specimens, I will then be able to interpret the results. The task could prove difficult, as this is a new drug and not much is known about its toxic and lethal blood concentrations. The process could take several days.

3:00 P.M. I return to my earlier case, as volunteers arrive and begin to eat the same crackers as those consumed by the driver of the car. I collect their urine afterward, and all of the samples test positive for morphine. This provides enough evidence to make a good case for the driver's defense.

5:45 P.M. I write a draft of my report on this case before leaving the office for the night. I will submit a full write-up to the police tomorrow.

CASE STUDY: The Fugitives

VICTIM Belle Elmore
CAUSE OF DEATH Hyoscine poisoning
WHERE London, England
WHEN January 31, 1910

The Crime

Dr. Hawley Harvey Crippen, a American doctor and ophthalmologist, moved to London with his second wife, a music-hall singer with the stage name Belle Elmore, in 1900. Unfortunately, his medical qualifications were not recognized in Britain and they depended heavily on Belle's money. Infatuated by the glamour of the theater, she had a series of open and flamboyant affairs, while keeping her husband under the tightest control. They rented a large Victorian house in Holloway, North London, and took in students, but Crippen returned home one day to find Belle in bed with one of the lodgers. The marriage finally fell apart, and Belle announced she was going to leave her husband, taking with her their joint savings. Soon after, she disappeared from the London scene.

The Case

The day after Belle had given a dinner party at their house on January 31, 1910, Crippen announced to her music-hall friends that she had left him and returned to America with one of her lovers. In the meantime, he moved his secretary and mistress, Ethel Le Neve, into the house, but several of Belle's friends became suspicious when she was seen wearing items of Belle's jewelry. The couple left London for Belgium, before taking a ship to North

America. Crippen had told the police that he had heard that Belle had died soon after arriving in America, and had already been cremated, which aroused their suspicions even further. With the couple away, the police searched the house on several occasions.

The Evidence

Only on the fourth search did they find the partial remains of a human body buried beneath the basement floor, but it was impossible to establish the identity immediately as the head, limbs, and most of the skeleton were missing. Finally the Home Office pathologist Sir Bernard Spilsbury was able to establish that the remains were those of Belle from a patch of abdominal skin bearing a healed scar from an operation. He also found traces of hyoscine, a poison which produced symptoms resembling those of heart failure, but which was used by doctors in small doses to relieve anxiety and travel sickness. All this evidence pointed directly at Crippen, and police began to hunt for the fugitive couple.

The Outcome

Crossing the Atlantic on the steamship *Montrose*, the couple were posing as father and son. The captain became suspicious at their unduly affectionate behavior and radioed a message to the police back in England. Chief Inspector Dew of Scotland Yard was able to catch a faster ship, which brought him to Canada before the *Montrose* docked. Boarding the ship off the Canadian coast, he arrested the couple. Both were put on trial for Belle's murder—Ethel Le Neve was acquitted, but Crippen was found guilty and hanged.

CASE STUDY: A Dose of Death

VICTIMS Mr. and Mrs. John Peck
CAUSE OF DEATH Germs and poison
WHERE New York, New York, United States
WHEN January to March 1916

occurred to Waite that it might be possible to give nature a helping hand, by causing Peck to ingest harmful bacteria, which would trigger an entirely convincing onset of a serious disease, followed by a severe physical decline and ultimate death, without anyone being held responsible.

The Crime

When the body of a possible murder victim is given a postmortem to determine the cause of death, one of the first signs examiners look for is the presence of any known poisons. This was known to Dr. Arthur Warren Waite, a dentist in New York, and he wondered, instead, whether it might be possible to harness germs spread by fatal diseases, so that his murders took on the appearance of death by natural causes. How could investigators then prove that the victims' demise was intentional?

Waite shared his luxury apartment on Riverside Drive with his wife's retired parents. His father-in-law, John Peck, had built up a sizeable fortune after a career as a pharmacist in the Midwest, and Waite longed to inherit as much of the money as possible. The problem was that neither parent seemed in poor health, but it

Waite kept samples of the diseases and germs he cultivated, and later used them to contaminate the prescriptions and food of his victims.

The Case

Waite began by setting his sights on John Peck's wife. He carefully isolated a mixture of diphtheria and influenza germs, and added these to her food. After a series of doses, the elderly woman became ill and her condition steadily deteriorated, until she died, in January 1916. Waite then shifted his efforts to her husband, but his method did not work so effectively on his second target. It seemed John Peck's constitution was disconcertingly immune to a whole range of nasty bugs, and every weapon was proving ineffective.

First he tried the diphtheria mixture, with no results. Then he prescribed a nasal spray to aid his victim's breathing, which he had contaminated with tuberculosis germs, but even this failed to produce the planned result. He tried influenza and typhoid, but still the old man remained stubbornly healthy. Finally, Waite's impatience overcame all the care and caution he had taken so far in his efforts. Determined to hasten his father-in-law's death, he added a dose of what he described to their family servant simply as "medicine" to tea and soup served to Peck one evening. The medicine did exactly what he hoped it would do. A man who had appeared to the family doctor as healthy only the day before, died on March 12, 1916, just two months after his late wife.

The Evidence

The medicine administered to the unfortunate John Peck was nothing less than a lethal dose of arsenic. Unluckily for the devious dentist, there was a reliable test for the presence of this poison, which had been developed by James Marsh, a London chemist, in the 1820s, and this was well known to the investigators. The first step of the test is to place tissue samples from the victim, together with any stomach contents, on to a zinc plate. Then sulfuric acid is poured on to the plate, and in the ensuing reaction any arsenic present in either tissue or stomach contents absorbs the hydrogen from the acid and is given off as a gas. This is collected and passed down a heated tube and then allowed to cool, where the mixture forms white crystals of arsenious oxide. When samples were taken from John Peck's body, the crystals showed exactly what Dr. Waite had turned to in his haste to be rid of his father-in-law.

The Outcome

With evidence as clear as this, the trial was something of a formality. Dr. Arthur Warren Waite was convicted of John Peck's murder, and before his execution he admitted the ingenious and successful methods he had used for poisoning his mother-in-law without incurring any suspicion at all. Had he persevered with these ideas, in time, Mr. Peck may have suffered the same fate as his wife without anyone being the wiser.

American doctor Arthur Warren Waite was convicted of the murders of Mr. and Mrs. Peck, in 1916. He poisoned the couple using bacteria from diseases to avoid suspicion.

CASE STUDY: A Deadly Cup of Tea

VICTIMS	Several family members
CAUSE OF DEATH	Thallium poisoning
WHERE	Sydney, Australia
WHEN	1947

The Crime

On the face of it, the death of 87-year-old Christina Mickelson in Sydney, Australia, in 1947 was hardly suspicious at all. When her friend Angeline Thomas died soon afterward, there seemed no cause for concern, as she too was in her 80s. However, the following year a younger relative, 60-year-old John Lundberg, fell seriously ill. His hair fell out, he became progressively weaker, and he was dead within weeks. By then, members of the Mickelson family were becoming seriously worried, and when Mary Ann Mickelson, also 60, fell ill and died with similar symptoms to Lundberg, their fears intensified.

The Case

Police looked for a common factor to link these deaths. They found one in a family member who had helped nurse all the family members before they died. Caroline Grills was 63 years old and had married Christina Mickelson's stepson, Richard Grills 40 years earlier. Now a grandmother and valued member of the extended family, her dowdy figure and thick-framed spectacles appeared regularly in their homes, bringing homemade cakes and cookies, and making endless cups of tea for her invalid charges. Though reluctant to cast suspicion on their "Aunt Carrie," the family could not help noticing that

Using a copper strip to test for the presence of thallium in a solution of hydrochloric acid and dissolved suspect body fluid or tissue.

whenever she failed to visit, the sickness would recede, only to reappear when she was back on duty.

The Evidence

The situation reached a crisis point. John Lundberg's widow, Eveline, and their daughter Christine Downey began to suffer from symptoms similar to those of their recently deceased relatives—extreme fatigue, difficulty in speaking and moving, loss of hair, and progressive blindness. One family member was worried enough to contact the police. The symptoms suggested a case of thallium poisoning, so a cup of tea, made for one of the victims, was analyzed. The results were clear, and the tea was indeed laced with

The Reinsch test is used to detect the presence of one or more heavy metals in a biological sample. The appearance of a silvery coating on the copper may indicate mercury. A dark coating indicates the presence of another metal, such as thallium.

A dark coating on the copper strip indicates the presence of thallium.

thallium. Caroline Grills was arrested so that the imminent danger to the victims was removed, but not before Eveline Lundberg lost her eyesight because of the poison. Police also took out an exhumation order to test the bodies of two of her earlier suspected victims, and both turned out to contain large enough quantities of thallium to confirm that they, too, had been poisoned. Thallium was a popular poison at the time, as it was the basis of a rat poison on the market. It was colorless, odorless, and tasteless, making it difficult for victims to realize there was anything sinister in what they were eating or drinking.

The Outcome

Caroline Grills was arrested and charged with the attempted murders of Eveline Lundberg and Christine Downey on May 11, 1953. These were the cases in which the evidence was strongest, since these were the victims for whom Grills had made the tea that had tested positive for thallium. She claimed her relatives had given evidence against her because of police pressure, but she was found guilty and sentenced to death on October 15, 1953. Six months later her appeal was turned down and her sentence was commuted to life imprisonment, but she only served six and a half years before she contracted peritonitis and died in hospital on October 6, 1960. Her motive for killing members of her family remained a mystery to the end. During her time in prison she proved extremely popular with other inmates, who nicknamed her "Aunt Thally."

CASE STUDY: Accidental Poisoning?

VICTIM Terence Armstrong
CAUSE OF DEATH Overdose of Seconal tablets
WHERE Gosport, Hampshire, England
WHEN July 22, 1955

The Crime

John and Janet Armstrong's son, Terence, was only five months old when he died on July 22, 1955, in Hampshire, near the naval hospital where his father served as a medic. It seemed that he had eaten the bright red berries of a laurel tree in the family's garden. The postmortem showed his stomach contained red skins similar to the berries, and the cause of this tragic and premature death appeared to be accidental—except that his brother, three-month-old Stephen, had died in the spring of 1954, and his three-year-old sister Pamela had been rushed to hospital just two months before Terence's death with an unexplained but serious illness that she only narrowly survived.

The Case

The pathologist who had carried out the postmortem exam, Dr. Harold Miller, had admittedly found what at first appeared to be shells of laurel berries in the baby's throat and stomach. He had placed one of these skins in a container of formaldehyde and the rest of the baby's stomach contents in another bottle and left both in the pathology laboratory refrigerator. When he examined them again later, he found the skins had dissolved, which suggested they were not natural berries at all.

The Evidence

Dr. Miller sent the samples, together with the baby's pillow and feeding bottle, to a specialist toxicology laboratory. They found that what had appeared to be berry skins were in reality traces of cornstarch and a red dye called eosin. The combination suggested the red gelatin-covered tablets of a powerful barbiturate called Seconal, so he dissolved some tablets of the drug in gastric juices. They broke down to produce the same residue as his samples.

Dr. Miller sent the samples to Scotland Yard's forensic laboratory where a long series of painstaking tests found minute samples of Seconal in the stomach contents and on the baby's pillow where he had vomited in his distress. Aware that the other two children had suffered similar symptoms in their illnesses, police exhumed the body of Stephen Armstrong, but found it was too decayed to reveal any specific poison. They also established that 50 Seconal tablets were missing from the hospital ward where John Armstrong worked, but there was still no proof that Seconal tablets had been brought to the house and given to the baby.

The Outcome

The truth was revealed a year later, when Janet Armstrong told police her husband had brought Seconal tablets home, and that after the baby's death, he had forced her to dispose of the rest of the tablets. Both were put on trial in November 1956. John Armstrong was sentenced to death for the murder of his son, and his wife was acquitted. A month later she admitted she had given Terence the fatal tablet, but by then her husband's sentence had been changed to life imprisonment.

CASE STUDY: Killer Painkillers

VICTIMS Susan Snow and
Bruce Nickell
CAUSE OF DEATH Cyanide poisoning
WHERE Seattle, Washington,
United States
WHEN June 11, 1986

The Crime

On the morning of June 11, 1986, Seattle bank employee Susan Snow died after taking two Excedrin extra-strength painkiller tablets for a persistent headache. At her postmortem, tests proved positive for cyanide poisoning. The logical explanation was that the painkillers had been contaminated with this deadliest of poisons, and when checked, cyanide traces were found in the remaining tablets.

The FDA and manufacturers Bristol-Myers recalled that batch of tablets. In the meantime, Seattle police checked local stores in the immediate area, and two more contaminated packs were found—one in the suburb where Susan Snow had lived, and the other a few miles away. The very next day, they were contacted by Stella Nickell, a recently widowed 42-year-old, whose husband Bruce had died after taking the same tablets 12 days earlier.

The Case

Tests showed two packs of Excedrin painkillers in Stella Nickell's home both contained cyanide traces. By then, searches over the northwestern United States had turned up only five contaminated packages, yet she insisted the two packets had been bought on different days from different stores. The odds against this defied any rational explanation, and Stella Nickell quickly moved from victim to potential suspect.

The Evidence

The FBI forensic laboratory checked the contaminated capsules more closely. Every one contained microscopic traces of a specialized chemical used to kill algae in tropical fish tanks. They identified a particular product called Algae Destroyer, and concluded the only reason for its presence was cross contamination, caused by the perpetrator of the crime preparing the cyanide in a container used to crush Algae Destroyer capsules.

There was still no positive link with Stella Nickell, but on August 25, detectives checking local pet supply stores found an assistant who identified Stella Nickell as a customer who had bought Algae Destroyer some weeks earlier. Police already knew the Nickells kept tropical fish, but at this stage the evidence was not conclusive enough to bring a case. Even when police discovered that the couple had been deeply in debt, and that Bruce had been heavily insured, Stella maintained her innocence.

The Outcome

Finally, one of the couple's daughters revealed she had heard her mother talk of killing her husband, and saying that cyanide might do the job very well, having researched the poison in books from local libraries. Agents found she had failed to return a book on poisons from the Auburn Library and had been sent an overdue notice for another book on poisonous plants. The book was traced and found to have been issued to her twice, shortly before her husband's death. Fingerprint checks revealed 84 of her prints, mostly on pages dealing with cyanide. Stella Nickell was charged with murder and product tampering, and on May 9, 1988, was sentenced to a total of 90 years in prison.

CASE STUDY: A Deadly Umbrella Attack

VICTIM Georgi Markov
CAUSE OF DEATH Ricin poisoning
WHERE London, England
WHEN September 7, 1978

cell count rose far above normal levels, and the doctors concluded he might be suffering from blood poisoning. He was given antibiotics, but before they could have any effect, he suffered severe convulsions. He sank into delirium and within three days he was dead.

The Crime

During the Cold War years, many dissidents from the Soviet Eastern European satellites found an apparently safe refuge in London. Some lived a quiet life in the West, but there were others who took a much more critical position against their former masters. One of these was Georgi Markov, a Bulgarian who worked for the BBC World Service, broadcasting to his former homeland.

On the afternoon of Thursday, September 7, 1978, Markov was waiting at a bus stop on Waterloo Bridge on the first stage of the routine journey back to his apartment. He felt a sudden stabbing pain in his right leg, and turned round to see that he had been jabbed by the end of a furled umbrella carried by a passerby. The man mumbled an apology, and rushed on to wave down a taxi.

When Markov reached his apartment, he took a closer look at the site of the pain and found a small red puncture mark in the skin of his leg. Thinking it would soon disappear, he went to bed unconcerned. But by the following day, he was violently sick and his temperature had risen sharply. He was taken to hospital, where his now inflamed wound was X-rayed, and he was kept under observation.

The X-ray showed no signs of anything to account for his illness, but his condition rapidly deteriorated. His pulse was racing as his blood pressure plummeted. His temperature fell, but his white blood

The Case

Markov's body was given a detailed postmortem examination, which revealed a tiny spherical pellet, only a millimeter or so across, buried beneath the skin. It had two very small holes drilled in it, but no sign remained of what it might have contained. The pellet was then sent to the Metropolitan Police forensic laboratory where it was analyzed and found to consist of an extremely tough alloy of platinum and iridium, which explained why it would not show up under X-ray. It was probable that the holes in the pellet had held a very small amount of poison, but no trace remained. On the other hand, to produce such a violent and lethal reaction suggested this must have been something like a nerve agent, and that the pellet itself had been fired into the victim's leg by a gas gun hidden within the furled umbrella.

The Evidence

The sophistication of the method and the poison used suggested that intelligence agents were responsible, rather than a criminal or terrorist group. The most likely poison was thought to be ricin, developed from the seeds of the castor oil plant. On entering the bloodstream it causes the red corpuscles to mass together and then attacks the other body cells, producing vomiting and high

Holes in tiny pellet contain poison.

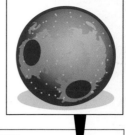

Pushing the trigger near the handle fired the pellet.

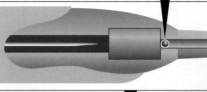

Gas cylinder made umbrella work like an air rifle.

A possible design of the umbrella gun that is suspected to have shot the pellet containing deadly ricin into Markov's leg.

temperature followed by falling blood pressure and eventually death from heart failure.

But could the microscopic dose of ricin contained in the pellet cause death so quickly? In the absence of any other proof, forensic experts carried out a comparison test. They injected a pig of similar size and weight to a mature human being with the amount of ricin that could have been contained within the holes in the pellet. Not only did the pig die within 24 hours, but the symptoms and organ damage that it suffered were similar to those experienced by Markov.

The Outcome

Suspicion pointed directly at the Bulgarian regime, which issued firm official denials. However, another Bulgarian dissident, Vladimir Kostov, had suffered a similar attack in Paris the year before. In his case, an identical pellet had been fired into his back where it lodged in the muscle tissues, but failed to penetrate any of the main blood vessels, so he survived the attack. But the final outcome of the story had to wait for the fall of the Communist regime in Bulgaria in 1991, and admission by the new government that their predecessors had commissioned and carried out assassination attempts against dissidents living in the West, including both Kostov and Markov.

CASE STUDY: 'Till Death Do Us Part

VICTIM Robert Curley

CAUSE OF DEATH Thallium poisoning

WHERE Luzeren County, Pennsylvania, United States

WHEN 1990 to 1991

The Crime

In August 1991, Pennsylvania electrician Robert Curley was admitted to hospital with a mysterious illness. He had leg pains, numbness, nausea, and burning in his hands and feet. His condition improved, however, and he was discharged on August 29. Nine days later, he was back and getting worse. On September 22, he recovered sufficiently to see his wife, brother, and sister, but that night he deteriorated and continued to do so until his wife agreed to the withdrawal of life support on September 27. By then, doctors had discovered high levels of thallium in his system and that they had led to his untimely death.

The Case

Curley had been working in a building that contained jars of thallium salts and, at first, it was thought that he had been accidentally exposed to the poison there. Tests showed that this was not possible, however. Moreover, the levels of thallium in his body could only have come from ingesting it through eating or drinking. One theory was that a fellow worker may have played a misguided prank on Curley by adding the thallium to his iced tea, thinking it was the similar-sounding Valium tranquilizer. Investigators interviewed his colleagues, but with no positive result. Since Curley had sought treatment, the case was ruled a homicide.

The Evidence

Years passed without any real progress. In 1994, however, a forensic toxicologist offered to produce a timeline indicating the peaks of thallium ingestion, which would give a clue as to how Curley had been exposed to the poison. The body was exhumed and samples taken of hair, nails, skin, and other tissues where thallium would be deposited. The analysis showed that the thallium levels in Curley's body began to rise in late 1990, then dropped, then rose and continued seesawing throughout 1991 until a final massive increase caused his death. It was puzzling that this had occurred even while he was in the hospital.

It became clear that Curley must have ingested the final dose on September 22, when he received visits from his family, and the finger of suspicion pointed at his wife. On his death, she had collected over $296,000 from an insurance policy. When investigators studied the peaks of thallium ingestion, they discovered that only Joann Curley had access to her husband on every occasion.

The Outcome

On July 17, 1997, Joann Curley admitted to murdering her husband with rat poison. The Curleys' marriage had been only a few months old when Joann began poisoning him because it had not turned out the way she thought it would. When asked why she didn't simply divorce him, she replied that she wanted the insurance money. She received a sentence of 10 to 20 years.

CASE STUDY: A Fatal Bedside Manner

VICTIMS At least 15 people
CAUSE OF DEATH Morphine overdose
WHERE Manchester, England
WHEN 1974 to 1998

The Crime

During the course of more than 20 years as a general practitioner in Manchester, England, numerous geriatric patients of Dr. Harold Shipman appeared to die from natural causes. Postmortems carried out on a number of exhumed bodies, however, showed that a good number of these people in fact died from a morphine overdose administered by the general practitioner, who curiously stood to benefit significantly from their deaths.

The Case

The body of Kathleen Grundy, an 81-year-old ex-mayor from Hyde, near Manchester, was found on a sofa in her home, on June 24, 1998. Her friends immediately called Dr. Harold Shipman, who had visited the house a few hours earlier and was the last person to see her alive (he said that he had been collecting samples for a survey on aging). Shipman pronounced her dead and the news was conveyed to Grundy's daughter, Angela Woodruff. The doctor told the daughter that an autopsy was unnecessary because he had seen Grundy shortly before her death.

However, following her mother's burial, Woodruff received a phone call from attorneys, who claimed to have a copy of her mother's will that left £386,000 ($556,000) to Dr. Shipman. Woodruff, believing it to be a forgery, went to her local police.

The Evidence

An autopsy was ordered and the body exhumed. Normal autopsy procedures were followed; blood, tissue, and hair samples taken from Ms. Grundy's body were sent to different labs for analysis. At the same time, police raided the doctor's home and offices, and found an old manual portable typewriter that Shipman told them he had sometimes lent to Grundy. Later, forensic scientists confirmed it was the machine used to type the counterfeit will and other fraudulent documents. Meanwhile, the toxicologist filed her report, showing that there was a lethal level of morphine in the dead woman's body and also that Grundy's death would have occurred within three hours of receiving the overdose.

The Outcome

Dr. Shipman's use of morphine was a miscalculation, since the drug is one of the few poisons that can remain in body tissue for centuries. He later claimed that Grundy was a morphine addict, but as past patients were exhumed and more autopsies were carried out, toxicologists found high levels of morphine in each of the bodies. The doctor was given consecutive life sentences for the murder of 15 people, although it is thought that his victims numbered more than 400. In January 2004, Shipman died in jail, apparently by suicide.

CASE STUDY: The Polonium Trail

VICTIM Alexander Litvinenko
CAUSE OF DEATH Polonium poisoning
WHERE London, England
WHEN November 2006

The Crime

Alexander Litvinenko was a prominent Russian defector living in London with his wife and teenage son. He had formerly worked for the KGB before the breakup of the Soviet Union, but had come under fierce criticism for failing to purge the intelligence service of corruption and links to organized crime. Since moving to the West, he had become an increasingly vocal critic of the leadership of Russian President Vladimir Putin, over what he saw as the erosion of freedom in his homeland. His outspoken claims of the Russian government's complicity in the deaths of other dissidents brought him an increasingly high-profile role in the London expatriate community, and he was known to have concerns about the possibility of action against him by the FSB, the KGB's successor as the Russian intelligence service.

The Case

On November 11, 2006, he was due to meet an Italian academic named Mario Scaramella at a Japanese sushi bar called Itsu. He planned to hand Scaramella information on the shooting of investigative journalist Anna Politovskaya in Moscow, and also to discuss rumors that both Litvinenko and Scaramella had appeared on a current FSB hit list. Later that day, he was due to meet three Russian

contacts in the Pine Bar of the Millennium Hotel: Vyacheslav Sokolenko, Dmitri Kowtun, and Andrei Lugovoi, all former KGB agents. Both meetings appeared to run according to plan, but that evening at his home in Muswell Hill, Litvinenko felt increasingly ill and was repeatedly sick. He was taken to hospital after three days of increasing stomach pains, where his condition continued to deteriorate. Three weeks after the onset of his mysterious symptoms, he was dead.

The Evidence

Following his death, tests on Litvinenko's body showed the presence of a highly toxic and unusual substance in his urine: polonium-210, a strong emitter of lethal alpha radiation if absorbed into a victim's body through the contamination of food or drink. Police found traces of the material at his home, and at the sites of both meetings. The net was spread more widely as traces showed up at both hospitals where Litvinenko had been treated, at the London office of exiled Russian business tycoon Boris Berezovsky, and on two airliners, which had carried out flights between Moscow and London. The use of polonium-210 carried several implications—it is quick and effective, but very easy to smuggle as its radiation is easily contained except when taken into the body. And it is almost impossible to procure, except for someone with the official power to obtain supplies from a nuclear power station or another working reactor.

The Outcome

At first, because of the contamination at the sushi bar, Scaramella came under suspicion until it

Alexander Litvinenko at the Intensive Care Unit of University College Hospital in London, on November 20, 2006.

emerged that Litvinenko had had a meeting with his Russian contacts there two weeks earlier. All the other signs therefore pointed to the Russian government, or at least the FSB, as they had the classic trilogy of motive (silencing an outspoken critic), means (access to nuclear reactors), and

opportunity (spiking Litvinenko's food or drink with the poison at one of several meetings). Furthermore, the Russian intelligence services have a long track record in assassinating those seen as enemies of the state, in a range of overseas countries. Meanwhile, applications have been made to extradite Andrei Lugovoi, but the Russians have refused, on the grounds that their constitution expressly forbids the extradition of Russian citizens. Lugovoi and his colleagues insist they are innocent of any involvement in the death of Litvinenko.

6

BITING THE BULLET

Guns and bullets can backfire on criminals when placed in the hands of ballistics experts. Depending on evidence found at the scene of a crime, firearms experts are able to determine invaluable information about the crime, the weapon used, and the likely suspect. A single bullet might indicate the kind of weapon used and the direction from which it was fired. A weapon left at the scene may reveal fingerprints or a serial number that leads investigators to its owner. A suspect apprehended after the crime may still have telltale gunshot residue on his or her hands.

CASE STUDIES:

- Martyrs or Murderers?
- Sabotage or Suicide?
- Passion or Premeditation?
- One Assassin or Two?
- Trigger Happy

The Smoking Gun

When there is evidence that a gun has been used at a crime scene, the investigators will call in a firearms examiner. This criminalist concentrates on four features of the scene: bullets, shell casings, signs of gunshot powder residue, and the weapon itself.

Handguns like this Beretta .40 pistol are often the weapon of choice, as they are easy to conceal and dispose of.

CHOOSE YOUR WEAPON

A gunshot wound can be inflicted by rifled firearms (revolvers, pistols, rifles, and machine guns) and nonrifled firearms (shotguns). In a rifled firearm, the inside of the barrel features spiral grooves, which cause the bullet to spin, stabilizing its flight. A nonrifled firearm has a smooth barrel. Handguns, rifles, and shotguns all produce very different and identifiable wound patterns.

ENTRY AND EXIT

If gunshot wounds are apparent on the body, no attempt is made to recover any bullets from wounds at the scene. They will be retrieved by the forensic pathologist during the postmortem examination. The pathologist will identify the entrance and exit wounds, and the path and direction of the bullet or bullets. These determinations are critical in establishing the manner of death. Key questions involve the wound size in relation to the weapon used; the estimated shooting range; and the relative positions of victim and perpetrator.

Scraping the Barrel

Investigators hand over a gun and bullets found at a crime scene. Firearms experts are asked to say whether a particular gun was used in the crime. What process do they follow?

1. A new bullet is test-fired through the gun into a tank filled with water or into cotton wadding, capturing the bullet without damaging it. This newly fired bullet now bears the gun's signature of scratches. When a bullet travels through a rifle barrel, the inside of the barrel scores a series of tiny scratches into it. The patterns of scratches are highly specific for particular types of gun, and are often sufficiently individual to link a bullet with a single weapon.

2. A comparison microscope is used to see if these marks match scratches on bullets found at the scene. The test bullet is examined and the most prominent set of scratches pinpointed. The other bullet is treated in the same way, the expert looking to see if the sets of scratches match.

3. Once the expert spots a possible match, he or she rotates both bullets in the same direction and at exactly the same rate to see if other markings come into view at the same time. If a low-power examination looks promising, the expert increases the magnification, and looks to see if smaller marks also line up.

4. It would be nice to think that this process is a precise science, but in reality there's a little skill involved. No two bullets ever look exactly the same. The bullet from the crime scene could have picked up additional markings when it struck the victim or anything else along the way. A gun barrel presents a different set of dust particles inside on each occasion it is fired, leaving differing marks on any bullet. Also, bullets themselves vary slightly in size, so each picks up its own unique set of marks as it travels down the barrel. It takes great expertise to conclude that two bullets almost certainly traveled down the barrel of one gun.

5. Useful information also comes from the shell case. The shape of the dent left by the firing pin on the shell case can vary from weapon to weapon, and examination can reveal a high probability that a particular gun was involved in a crime. In addition, when a gun fires, the explosion forces the shell case against the back of the chamber, and any imperfections in the chamber become stamped into the shell. If the firearm is an automatic or semi-automatic weapon, the mechanism that loads and removes the shell also leaves characteristic marks. While this information is useful, it has less power than evidence found on the bullet—the fact that you have found a shell case linked to a gun at a crime scene does not in itself prove that a particular person was guilty of the offense.

FROM BULLET TO CRIMINAL

The idea of linking a person to a crime by showing that he or she once held the gun has a long history. While performing an autopsy in 1794, a surgeon found a wad of paper buried in a bullet wound. Guns in those days were muzzle-loaders, and the wad would have been used to pack the bullet and gunpowder into the gun before firing. When unfurled, the wad turned out to have been torn from a sheet of music. Later a suspect was arrested, and in his pocket was the rest of the same sheet of music. The man was soon hanging from the local gallows.

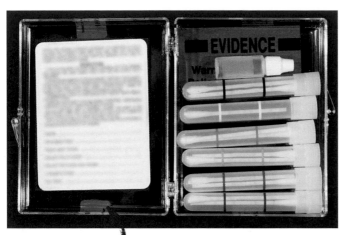

An atomic absorption kit used for testing gunshot residue.

In modern guns, the ammunition consists of a bullet that is pointed at the front and flat at the base. The base is held by a hollow shell case that is packed with gunpowder. In the rear of the case is a small amount of primer that ignites when the gun's firing pin dents the case. The bullet then flies off, and the shell case is held inside the gun or, in the case of some automatic loading systems, ejected.

Over the years, forensic ballistics experts have developed an increasingly sophisticated battery of tests that enable them to link bullets with specific guns, and guns with specific people. For example, when Frederick Parmenter, paymaster of the Slater and Morrill Shoe Factories in the town of South Braintree, Massachusetts, was shot dead on April 15, 1920, suspect Nicola Sacco's pistol was positively linked with a bullet found in body, although no other evidence could place Sacco at the scene of the crime (see page 130).

A range of bullets, each one displayed in its complete state and as it would typically appear after test-firing into a water tank.

GUNPOWDER GIVEAWAY

On many occasions gunpowder residues can yield valuable
information. The pattern of residue can give a strong indication of
how far the gun was from the target when the shot was fired. This
sort of evidence can be useful if the suspect is claiming self-defense,
as it will show how close he or she was to the victim. In cases of
suspected suicide, careful examination shows highly characteristic
patterns indicating that the weapon was held very close. The absence
of these marks would raise deep suspicions of foul play.

These assessments have most use in court if the suspect's actual
weapon can be used to produce a similar pattern of marks on a test

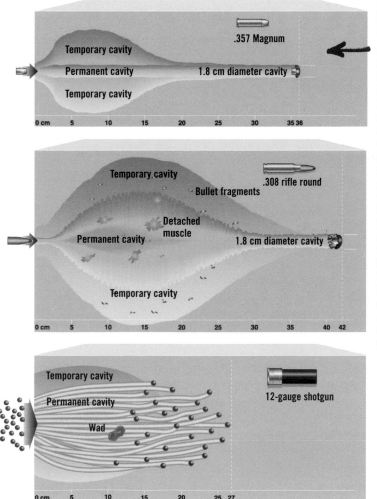

Comparison of the Effects of Three Common Bullet Types

A bullet perforates the skin
in 50 nanoseconds. At first
the skin stretches as the
bullet disrupts the epidermal
layer, and the energy wave
results in lacerations of
capillaries and small vessels
within the subepidermal
layer. The cavity in the tissue
is caused as the bullet and
gases compressing the
neighboring tissue pass
through it. This cavity lasts
for about three nanoseconds.
After the cavity contracts,
it is rimmed with
hemmorrhaging tissue.
This basic sequence can
be affected by the type of
weapon, the type of
ammunition, and the
distance from the end of
the muzzle to the skin.

surface. If investigators have not recovered a weapon, any comments will always have to be restricted to best guesses based on any previous experience they may have.

A Question of Distance

Firing from less than ³/₄ of an inch (2 cm) leaves a heavy

concentration of residue immediately around the bullet wound, and if the bullet has passed through clothing, the edges may be scorched or melted. Fabric can also be torn in a four-pointed star, created by gasses rushing back into the barrel immediately after the shot is fired. Holding the gun 12 to 16 inches (30 to 40 cm) away leaves scattered specks of burned and unburned powder, while shots fired from up to 3 feet (1 m) away can leave traces of powder on the target.

A suspect's hand is swabbed to gather gunshot residue and determine the presence of cordite, which is often used in gun cartridges as a propellant.

An expert can still collect some residue even if the attacker was standing a mile or more away and using a high-powered rifle. This is because the bullet is coated with a small quantity of dust that is wiped off as it enters the victim, and which can be collected by wiping carefully around the bullet's point of entry.

Areas of Concentration

In the case of smooth-bore weapons that fire shot instead of individual bullets, the farther the target is from the gun, the greater the spread of the shot. When held closer than about 6 feet (2 m), the shot will be in one concentrated zone just a little wider in diameter than the gun's bore. As a rule of thumb, the diameter of the impact zone increases by about 1 inch (2.5 cm) for every additional 3 feet (1 m) of separation.

Key Ingredients

Evidence doesn't only come from the victim. Swabbing a suspect's hands within a few hours of an offense, particularly the webbed region between thumb and forefinger, may detect chemical traces that will show whether he or she recently held or fired a gun. Ballistics experts then use neutron activation analysis or atomic absorption spectrophotometry to find traces of barium, lead, and antimony, which are used in the primer. In some cases, a scanning electron microscope is used to show minuscule details, in which case samples

Ballistics on File

As with so many areas of forensics, computers are increasingly helping ballistics experts. Law enforcement agencies use powerful systems to examine individual bullets and compare them with previously recorded evidence stored in a database—in a fraction of the time it would take to do the same task without computers.

The FBI's DRUGFIRE database holds digitized images of cartridge cases. The integrated ballistic identification system (IBIS) developed for the U.S. Bureau of Alcohol, Tobacco, Firearms, and Explosives (ATF), carries digital images of both cartridges and bullets. In 1999, staff from the FBI and the ATF merged their two systems to create NIBIN, the National Integrated Ballistic Information Network. This drew together the individual strengths of each platform. The equipment allows firearms technicians to grab digital images of markings and let the computer make an initial search through the database. In seconds it can check against hundreds of thousands of records. The computer lists the most likely comparisons, and firearms examiners then check these.

are taken using specially made adhesive-coated aluminum discs. Different manufacturers of bullets use different gunpowder recipes when making up the explosive in each bullet.

Analyzing the chemicals in the residue and comparing the results with a reference database may uncover the manufacturer of the offending bullet. Interpreting the evidence is not a straightforward task. If there's no residue present on a person's hands, it could mean that they didn't fire the weapon, that they wore a glove, or that the gun had a particularly clean firing action. On the other hand, finding residue on a person's palm, but not between thumb and forefinger, may mean that the suspect picked up the gun after it had been fired, rather than pulling the trigger himself.

NUMBER REVELATIONS

Every gun has its own serial number, which the authorities use to record ownership of individual weapons. Criminals often grind off these numbers to hide a firearm's original identity—but traces are sometimes left behind and the numbers can be restored. When a number is stamped into a gun, the metal below each character is stressed, making it fractionally weaker than the surrounding area. With care, an expert can often use etching solutions, such as mixtures of hydrochloric acid and copper chloride, to dissolve this stressed metal, and re-establish the serial number. If revealed, the number is photographed immediately, as the etching process may continue and erase it completely.

TELLING THE STORY

A firearms investigator's first job at a crime scene is to try to work out how many shots were fired. It may be that witnesses can help by recalling the number of "bangs" they heard, and this can be confirmed if spent cartridges or bullets are found. Recovering the weapon is a huge step forward, and this too can give clues about the number of shots fired, as the number of unused cartridges still inside can be counted.

The next task is to find the bullets. Some of these may well be inside the victim, and taking X-ray images of his or her body will find them, or fragments of them. Often the bullets recovered from the scene of a crime are so badly squashed or mangled that markings aren't visible. Even so, locating the bullets can help investigators trace where the gun was when it was fired. Inserting rods or shining laser pointers through bullet holes in furniture, walls, or any other item in the area can also help point toward the gun's location. It was by following such steps—analyzing the timing of shots recorded during a 911 call, and producing computer-generated visuals to show the location from which each shot was fired—that police investigators were able to determine whether or not the 1991 murder of Artie Mitchell had been premeditated or not (see page 134).

On occasion, forensic investigators may even make up a mannequin to represent the victim, complete with bullet holes that relate to his or her injuries. This can be particularly useful if more than one gun was involved and multiple shots were fired, as it can begin to show which shots were discharged from which weapon.

Discovering that a bullet ricocheted off the floor, walls, or furniture can make a huge difference to any investigation. It may be that the gun was facing away from the victim and fired accidentally, or as a warning shot with no intention of harming a person, but a sequence of chance bounces made it strike the victim. The defense team may well use this type of evidence to claim that the lesser charge of manslaughter would be more appropriate than murder.

Dr. David Pryor

Chief Consultant Forensic Scientist with Forensic Access Ltd, London, UK

A typical day involves processing operational casework submissions relating to firearms and ammunition. Lab-based work includes the examination of exhibits, microscopy of bullets and cartridge cases, and collating all the results into an expert witness report.

9:00 A.M. I've just arrived at the lab and a call comes in from the crime scene manager (CSM) informing us that a shooting has occurred. There is one deceased and the body is still in situ. A ballistics scientist is required to meet the pathologist and other scene examiners at the location and help interpret the circumstances.

10:00 A.M. I arrive at the scene and meet the pathologist. The senior investigating officer (SIO) and CSM brief us as to the circumstances as understood at the time. The pathologist and I examine the body for any external evidence of gunshot injury, taking meticulous notes as we go along. I also search the scene for firearms-related evidence, such as cartridge cases and bullets that may have exited or missed the bodies. Having satisfied himself that all necessary samples have been taken from the body, the pathologist authorizes the removal of the body from the scene. The pathologist and I brief the SIO as to our findings so far.

12 NOON I arrive at the mortuary. The body is already in the process of being X-rayed to locate any bullets. I observe the postmortem and discuss the wound ballistics with the pathologist and SIO. When a bullet is recovered, it is washed and dried and I can then examine it and give my preliminary assessment as to caliber, weapon type, and, in some cases, a possible make of gun. Relevant samples are logged into the exhibit book with a

unique identifying mark, as continuity is paramount. The SIO suspects that this shooting is linked to other offenses, so he requests an urgent laboratory examination of the recovered material.

3:00 P.M. I arrive back at the laboratory and book the samples in. First, I examine those that are not required for other disciplines, such as fingerprints and DNA. Initial notes and photographs are made and I can then proceed to the microscopy of the samples, looking for both class characteristics that will help me identify the weapon type and unique details that will allow me to determine how many guns were used. If relevant samples are available to me, then I will engage the services of a technician to load the samples via a digital capture microscope and to run a correlation against a national database of unsolved crimes. If the weapon has been used before, then a "hit" should appear in the correlation list. I will then be able to confirm the match using comparison optical microscopy.

4:30 P.M. A match is confirmed and, after a quality assurance check by a fellow examiner, the SIO is informed. I then write a short report on my findings from that day. This will be followed up, after full laboratory examinations, by a complete witness statement, including results from the examination of other material that has been submitted as additional to the first exhibits.

CASE STUDY: Martyrs or Murderers?

VICTIMS Frederick Parmenter and Alessandro Beradelli

CAUSE OF DEATH Gunshot wounds

WHERE South Braintree, Massachusetts, United States

WHEN April 15, 1920

The Crime

Frederick Parmenter was paymaster of the Slater and Morrill Shoe Factories in the town of South Braintree, Massachusetts. On April 15, 1920, he was carrying more than $15,000 in payroll envelopes from one building to another some 200 yards (180 m) away, with security guard Alessandro Beradelli, when they passed two men dressed in dark clothing. One of them tried to grab Beradelli, and the other pulled out a gun and shot Parmenter twice and Beradelli five times, killing both men. A Buick sedan containing two other men pulled up and, joined by a lookout, all five piled the cash into the vehicle and drove off at high speed. All that police found at the scene were spent cartridge cases of three different makes: Peters, Remington, and Winchester.

The Case

The getaway automobile was found in nearby woods. Police were able to link it to a failed robbery at another shoe factory in nearby Bridgewater, involving a criminal named Mike Boda. He owned the same model of Buick, as well as an Overland, left for repairs at a garage in the village of Cochesett. The police asked the garage owners to call them when Boda came to collect the automobile. On May 5, he arrived with a friend on a motorcycle and two other associates, named Nicola Sacco and Bartolomeo Vanzetti, arrived on foot. By the time the police

reached the scene, all four had left. Sacco and Vanzetti had caught a streetcar to Brockton. They were picked up at an intermediate stop, and searched. Both men were armed: Sacco with a .32 Colt automatic and a pocket full of bullets, and Vanzetti with a .38 Harrington & Richardson revolver.

The Evidence

Both men appeared to resemble eyewitness descriptions, but both denied any involvement and they had convincing alibis. The crucial evidence was a .32 bullet found in Beradelli's body. The cartridges in Sacco's pocket were of the same type, and these were used for test firings to produce a comparison. When the test bullets were compared under a microscope with the one found in the victim's body, the minute scratches and scorings caused by the rifling in the barrel of the gun provided a perfect match.

Both men were convicted of murder and sentenced to death, but the case proved controversial from the outset. A self-proclaimed ballistics expert named Alexander Hamilton claimed the ballistics evidence was false, and a retrial was requested. Though his evidence at an earlier trial had nearly convicted an innocent man, Hamilton was allowed to make his case to the court. He brought in two Colt revolvers and dismantled them, together with Sacco's gun. It was only when he was caught trying to reassemble the barrel of the murder weapon onto one of his Colt pistols that the retrial was quashed. Later, Calvin Goddard of the Bureau of Forensic Ballistics in New York was able to demonstrate the closeness of the match between bullets, which proved that, although no cartridges had been found at the scene of the crime, the gun found in Sacco's pocket at the time of the arrest had definitely killed the security guard.

The Outcome

Sacco and Vanzetti had no clear criminal connections, but they were known to be anarchists at a time when the authorities were worried by such groups advocating a violent overthrow of society. Their supporters claimed that they were being executed for their political beliefs and many celebrities joined a campaign for their acquittal. They were executed on August 23, 1927, but in 1977 the Governor of Massachusetts issued what amounted to a proclamation of innocence. A team of forensic experts reexamined the evidence in 1961 and again in 1983. Both times the ballistics evidence was confirmed as accurate, but what no one could prove was whether Sacco had been the person firing the gun on that fatal day.

Bullets and casings from the Sacco and Vanzetti trial. The top row below are the bullets removed from the victim's body.

CASE STUDY: Sabotage or Suicide?

VICTIMS 47 sailors
CAUSE OF DEATH Explosion
WHERE Caribbean Sea
WHEN April 19, 1989

The Crime

Each of the four huge battleships of the Iowa class of the U.S. Navy carried nine 16-inch (406-mm) guns in three triple turrets, which could fire a high-explosive projectile weighing 1¼ tons up to 24 miles (40 km). To propel the huge shells, the turret crews had to load different combinations of bagged nitro-cellulose explosive charges into the breech of the gun behind the shell.

USS *Iowa* was carrying out a practice firing on April 19, 1989, when explosive charges being loaded into the breech of the center gun of number two turret suddenly detonated. The explosion sent a blast back through the turret, killing 47 sailors. Navy investigators had to determine whether the disaster was accidental or sabotage.

The Case

The gun had not been fired recently, so there was no possibility of heat buildup, and the investigation established that a spontaneous explosion in a cold

barrel had never occurred in the history of the Navy. Investigators found traces of steel wool, calcium hypochlorite, and brake fluid inside the barrel. Could they be the remains of a device placed there to set off the charges? The captain of the center gun, Clayton Hartwig, was rumored to have had a relationship with a sailor in the turret crew, and had been in control of the loading operation. Both men died in the tragedy; could it have been a bizarre act of suicide or revenge?

The Evidence

Explosives experts carried out a second technical investigation. First, they checked the gun turrets of

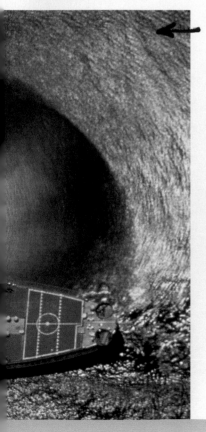

The USS *Iowa* firing her guns during target practice before the disaster happened.

the Iowa's sister ships, where they found similar traces of steel fibers, calcium, and chlorine in barrels that had been fired with no trouble. Tests showed they are found in cleaning fluids and lubricants used in turret maintenance and were not evidence of sabotage.

One factor separated the loading of the center gun from those on either side, which functioned normally. The power-driven rammer which forced the bagged charges into the breech, pushed them two feet (0.6 m) further than it should have, with greater force. However, explosive charges remain stable under heavy provocation. Setting light to the explosive with a cigarette lighter took nine minutes, and dropping the charges from heights of up to 100 feet (30 m) caused no problem.

Then the experts examined the "trim bags"— additional bags of explosive inserted into the main charges to correct weight variations. Unlike the main charges, the explosives in the smaller bags were not tightly packed, making them potentially more susceptible to the shock of over-ramming when the gun was loaded. They set up a test rig and dropped a series of charges to replicate these effects. Nothing happened in 17 successive tests, but when it was dropped for the 18th time, the charge was loaded with fewer trim-charge pellets with wider gaps between them and this time the charge finally detonated and blew the test rig apart.

The Outcome

Supplied with an explanation of a technical fault for the explosion, the Navy was able to take action in changing the loading procedures for its biggest guns, and no more firing mishaps were identified.

CASE STUDY: Passion or Premeditation?

VICTIM Artie Mitchell
CAUSE OF DEATH Gunshot wounds
WHERE Corte Madera, California, United States
WHEN February 27, 1991

The Crime

James and Artie Mitchell were brothers who ran a successful business making pornographic films. Their productions were technically poor, entirely explicit, cheap to make, and enormously lucrative. One reportedly cost $60,000 to make but earned $25 million. However, the brothers were having a succession of arguments that were becoming louder and more violent. By 1991, with Jim now aged 48 and Artie, 46, their earnings and their differences reached their peak. At 10:15 P.M. on the night of February 27, Artie's girlfriend, Julie Bajo, called 911. Not only did she report a shooting, but the operator could clearly hear shots being fired, a fact later confirmed on the recordings that are routinely made of emergency calls.

The Case

When police turned up at Artie's house in Corte Madera, they found Jim Mitchell outside, apparently dazed by what had happened. He was holding a small-bore .22 rifle and had a .38 handgun in a shoulder holster, though this had not been fired. Inside they found the body of Artie lying in the bedroom and they found eight cartridge cases, although there were only three obvious bullet wounds—one in the abdomen, one in his right arm, and the third in his right eye. There was no need to

prove that Jim Mitchell had fired the shots: ballistics evidence would have confirmed it, but he freely admitted having done so. But what was his motive?

Those who knew the brothers well insisted that as the older brother, Jim had taken care of Artie throughout the years the two had been growing up and prospering in business together. Only the year before, Jim had risked his life by going into rough sea on a surfboard to rescue Artie and one of his sons, and effectively saved them from drowning. So the most difficult question was, did the shooting of Artie Mitchell represent a case of premeditated murder or was it an all-consuming outburst of rage, which might make it a case of manslaughter?

The Evidence

The tape recording of the telephone conversation proved vital in trying to make a case for premeditated murder, since it established the time intervals between each of the shots. Though only five shots were heard during the emergency telephone call, it was almost certain the first three had been fired before the call was connected and the recording began. Of the five on the recording, the most significant were shots three and four, which occurred with a gap of almost half a minute between them. The prosecution was trying to establish that this length of gap would have allowed someone suffering from anger time to reflect on what was happening, and to stop. To resume after such an interval was, they said, clear evidence of premeditation and intent, hence the crime was murder. For the first time, crime scene experts used the evidence of where they had found the bullets to construct a three-dimensional computer-generated image of the shootings, ending with Artie being killed by the shot through his eye. This was seen by experts on the defense team as being a step too far, as it depended on too many assumptions about which shot was which in the sequence of sounds.

The Outcome

Jim Mitchell went on trial for his brother's murder 11 months after the shooting. His defense counsel undermined the prosecution reconstruction of the crime so effectively that the jury threw out the murder charge and on February 18, 1992, he was found guilty of manslaughter and sentenced to six years' imprisonment. After serving almost his entire sentence, he was released on parole on October 3, 1997.

James Mitchell confers with his lawyer, Michael Kennedy, during his trial for murdering his brother and business partner, Artie Mitchell.

CASE STUDY: One Assassin or Two?

VICTIM John F. Kennedy
CAUSE OF DEATH Gunshot wound
WHERE Dallas, Texas, United States
WHEN November 22, 1963

The Crime

On November 22, 1963, U.S. President John F. Kennedy was shot and fatally wounded while driving though the city of Dallas, Texas, in a motorcade. Lee Harvey Oswald was arrested for the murder, but many suspected that he didn't act alone. The question remains to this day: How many people were involved? One aspect of speculation is that Kennedy was not the only person hit; a bullet also struck Governor John Connally as he traveled in the president's car.

The Case

The autopsy had been superficial and the investigation incomplete. When the old files were investigated, it was discovered that certain key items were missing: photographs of President Kennedy's internal chest wounds, glass slides

of his skin wound, and Kennedy's brain. The Warren Commission, set up to investigate the shooting, concluded that Oswald fired three bullets. One missed and was lost. One hit the president in the back before going on to strike the governor. One struck the president in his head. But critics of the commission are skeptical that a single bullet wounded both the president and the governor. Doesn't it make more sense, they ask, to say that the wounds attributed to a single bullet were a result of two bullets fired from different places?

The Evidence

To try to answer these doubts, forensic scientists in 1979 used neutron activation analysis to analyze the metal in the two recovered bullets and in several metal fragments taken from the two men's wounds. The analysis focused on the metals, silver, and antimony, in the bullet pieces that are present in tiny amounts. These trace elements vary considerably from bullet to bullet, but are very similar in pieces of metal from a single slug.

The Outcome

The results showed two distinct clusters of trace elements, with some bullet pieces belonging to one cluster, the rest to the other. This indicated that a single bullet had wounded both men; the other bullet had hit Kennedy only. The experts concluded that there was no reason to disbelieve the Warren Commission's conclusions.

Although the two bullets that wounded Kennedy had minor differences in composition, they were almost certainly fired from the same gun.

CASE STUDY: Trigger Happy

VICTIMS Four people
CAUSE OF DEATH Gunshot wounds
WHERE West Palm Beach, Florida, United States
WHEN 2004

The Crime

A shooting incident outside a Palm Beach restaurant on November 4, 2004, involving a pair of gunmen, caused the deaths of two men—Reynold Barnes and Eddie Lee Gibbs. Just three days later, a vehicle carrying three men— Larry Turner, Ali Jean, and Turner Norwood—was riddled with bullets in a drive-by shooting in the same area. Turner was injured but survived, while his two companions died at the scene. Cartridge casings were found at both scenes, showing that three different guns had been used in the murders. One of them, a Glock automatic pistol, was used in both incidents.

The Case

The casings were examined, and photographed using a special camera system called BrassTRAX, which reveals the unique markings pressed into the case when the gun is fired. The images were then sent to the NIBIN database for analysis and comparison with the records of other guns in its records. The search found one perfect match: a Glock that had been stolen from a police deputy. The cartridge data also matched cartridges retrieved from other shooting incidents in the area, dating back to late summer 2004. But who had been pulling the trigger?

The Evidence

Cartridges from the stolen gun had been found at the scene of a shooting at another local restaurant in August. No one died, and security camera footage clearly showed the identity of the man firing the weapon, a known criminal named Derek Dixon. Other matching cartridges came from a shooting at a nightclub on September 25.

Finally, on December 3, 2004, shots were fired outside an Arby's Restaurant in Palm Beach Gardens in a botched automobile theft. A gun was dropped at the scene which proved to be the missing Glock. Dixon was arrested as a suspect, and in January 2005 was also charged on four counts of second-degree murder. The NIBIN database, the security footage, and the attempted automobile theft showed he had used the gun both before and after the fatal shootings, and police also had the evidence of a codefendant, backed up by a recorded confession taken from Dixon while he was in custody in the county jail. He had alleged the intended victims at the August shootings were the people he killed on November 4. The later shooting was to kill Larry Turner, whom Dixon believed had tried to kill his brother. He had traded some stolen jewelry with the criminal who had taken the deputy's gun in July 2004 to secure the Glock for himself.

The Outcome

In March 2005, Dixon pleaded guilty to all four counts of second-degree murder, and to the car theft charges as well as to the offense of possession of a handgun by a convicted felon. He was sentenced to forty years for the murders, and another forty years, to be served concurrently, for the other charges.

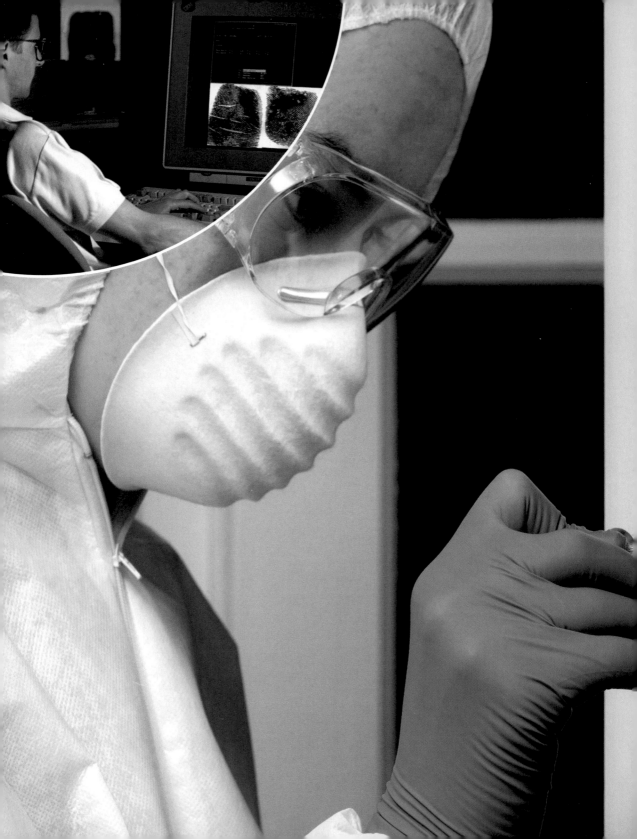

7

MAKING AN IMPRESSION

It is practically impossible to disappear from the scene of a crime without leaving any physical trace. Criminals may be clever enough to wear gloves or masks to obscure their identities—although this is not always the case—but they may also have little knowledge of just how little evidence is required by investigating officers seeking to link them to a crime. A bite from a discarded apple, tool marks found at the scene, and footprints left in mud or snow are just some of the ways that criminals have been brought to justice.

CASE STUDIES:
- Anatomy of Murder
- A Mass Fingerprinting
- Trail of a Serial Killer
- The Jagged Tooth
- The Killing of Kevin Jackson
- A Matter of Inheritance

Telltale Marks

A footprint found at a crime scene is marked off by investigators, ready for a cast to be made for further analysis at the lab.

A mark or impression is either a two-dimensional image on a flat surface, such as a footprint on a dusty wooden floor, or a three-dimensional impression, such as a tire track in snow or mud.

WORKING FROM THE INSIDE OUT

Finding marks can be tricky, partly because first responders and investigators alike easily destroy them unintentionally. As a precaution against this, investigators work from the outer edges of the crime scene inward toward the center. Markings can also be difficult to see if they are made on a hard surface.

Once a potential location of a marking is spotted, it is time to get out the brush and fingerprint powders. The task of enhancing a marking is often more difficult than with fingerprints, because, unlike fingers, synthetic articles such as shoes and tires do not leave behind oils and proteins to which dust easily adheres; they just rearrange the material they are on. Many of the criminalist's dyes and dusts won't help here.

FOOTPRINT FINDINGS

Deep impressions made by footwear in materials such as mud, snow, and sand can be very valuable to an investigation because they show high levels of detail. Technicians take measures to create the most accurate prints possible.

Measures Taken

- **Water** Taking a print that is waterlogged can prevent an accurate cast being made. Unmixed dental cement is often used to absorb the water, and the cast is then topped up with ready-mixed cement.

- **Environment** Inclement weather and the environment can thwart efforts to get information from deep prints. A footprint in sand will blow away unless dealt with quickly. Hair spray is often sprayed over the print to help bind it, thus giving time to pour a casting material into the print.

- **Snow** Tracks in snow are obviously prone to melting and must be handled carefully. Snow itself can be stabilized a little with a material called Snow Print Wax, but the print will still need casting. Dental cement takes longer to set when cold, and also gives off heat, but it's the only option. To try to get a good cast, the cement is used cold and poured in slowly to maximize the chance that the heat will dissipate through the snow without melting the print.

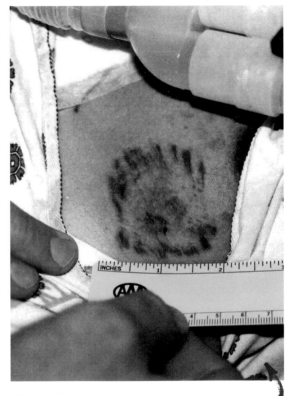

A suspected bite mark on a victim is photographed immediately with a scale before the impression has the chance to fade.

SPOT THE DIFFERENCE

Police investigators call on computer power in some situations, for example, when they can't see a footprint on a relatively clean surface but suspect that one is there. One option is to take a photograph of the area, wash down the area thoroughly, and then take a second photograph from exactly the same place as the first. When these photographs are fed into a computer, image analysis software can be used to remove extraneous background information (such as scratches on a wooden floor) and look for differences between the two photographs. These differences could be an indication of traces of the footprint.

Forensic investigators used this technique in Toronto, Canada, to search for a footprint on a shop counter after an assault by a young man. They revealed a print from a size 12 Converse sneaker. Faint though it was, the suspect had made his mark.

Marking Progress

When marks or prints are found, the investigator acts as follows:

- A forensic photographer takes photos of the prints, placing a ruler in the shots so that size is recorded.
- If the prints form a sequence, the distance between prints is measured to give clues about a person's height, as well as how fast he or she was moving. Even if the prints don't provide much detail, they can still be useful, as they may lead investigators toward areas of the crime scene that need to be given special attention.
- If a tire mark is found, criminalists look for the one from the opposite side of the vehicle. The distance between the two tracks and the width of each tread mark can indicate the sort of vehicle that created it.
- Tool marks, such as those left after prying open a window with a screwdriver, can also be molded. This time, the item will have to be taken back to the lab, as the impression is usually on a vertical surface and cannot be cast as it stands. When making relatively small casts it is best to insert the spatula used for stirring the cement into the material as it sets. This way, it will become locked into the cast, giving both a handle with which to remove the cast and a label.

As with fingerprints, these markings can link different crimes together. Databases list prints from almost any article you can imagine—shoes, tires, screws, and so on. These databases contain not only data from crime scenes, but also records of different manufacturers' products, so a shoeprint can easily reveal the make and size of the person's shoe, giving valuable additional information about just who investigators should be looking for.

Crime scene investigators photograph a deep print found at the scene before a cast is made.

All Fingers and Thumbs

No two fingerprints belonging to a single person are alike, and no two people share the same prints. Moreover, a person's prints are permanent throughout life; record them at birth and you'll be able to identify the same person in his or her nineties. These facts have made fingerprinting an extremely important tool in crime detection.

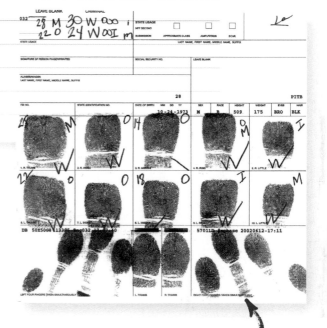

A full set of fingerprints, showing each digit separately, as well as all four fingers together.

WHAT'S IN A PRINT?

At a crime scene, prints fall into one of three broad categories, depending on how easy it is to see them:

- **Patent prints** Patent prints can be seen by just looking; they are the type that were made because a person's hand was covered in something like ink, oil, or blood, and the mark is clearly visible. To collect one of these, a criminalist often simply needs to take a careful close-up photograph.
- **Latent prints** This type of fingerprint cannot be seen until you have enhanced it with a powder or chemical reagent.
- **Impressed prints** These are prints that have been pressed in a soft material such as congealed blood, mud, or snow. Forensics experts may be able to capture impressed prints by photographing them, or by casting a molding.

DATA BASICS

In the days before computerization, the information gleaned from fingerprints was kept on individual cards in the form of vast filing systems. Finding a match between a print from a crime scene and anyone on file was time-consuming, as investigators would have to sift through thousands of cards. Even though there are ways to narrow the search, with the cards being sorted by such characteristics as sex; age; presence of scars; presence of whorl, loop, and arch formations in various fingers; and ridge counts and tracings, you might at best have found that you have a quarter of the cards to sort through, rather than the entire fingerprint filing system. Computers have vastly sped up the search process. In the first mass-fingerprinting case in the UK, in 1948, it took police over two months to search through 45,000 fingerprints (see page 149). Current systems can perform 40,000 searches each day if necessary.

Computerized fingerprint systems now scan prints picked up at crime scenes and automatically plot the relative positions of features such as the places where ridges divide in two. They also note the angle between different ridges. Once this data is stored numerically, it is easy for the computer to search its database looking for potential matches. It's then down to a fingerprint expert to scrutinize the prints from possible suspects to see if the computer got it right.

This computerized analysis has another advantage besides speed. It can work on the assortment of partial prints often recovered from a

A forensic scientist uses a computer to compare fingerprints found at a crime scene with those of a suspect on the database.

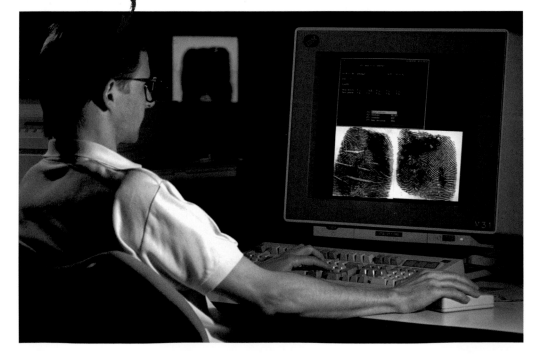

The Perfect Print

Getting a latent print takes time and practice. A fingerprint examiner uses delicate brushes to gently layer powder over a print. Dusting powders of various different types and color are the classic means of making latent prints visible. Some powders are fluorescent and are useful on multicolored surfaces, as the print can be made to shine in UV light.

Evidence collected from a crime scene is dusted with fluorescent powder and viewed under ultraviolet light to look for fingerprints.

1. Prints are so fragile that even the softest brush could destroy them. The fingerprint examiner gently shakes or twirls the brush just above where the print is thought to be. Once it starts to come into view, the examiner builds up layers of dust, each time moving the brush in the direction of the lines in the print. Excess dust is cleared with compressed air.

2. The print is photographed and lifted onto a card. Lifting tape may be used for single prints. This process needs a steady hand, because the tape must be placed straight down on the print without wrinkles or bubbles. The tape needs to be pulled away in one long smooth movement and carefully laid on a card. Each print is given a number. The location of the print is also recorded, in a map or diagram of the scene. Sometimes there may be enough dust left in the print that the expert can repeat this process and lift it for a second time. The advantage is that this second lift may give a clearer view of certain details within the print.

3. On some surfaces, a print is so fragile that it has to be stabilized before it can be enhanced with dust. Experts often use the cyanoacrylic chemicals in superglue for this purpose. A small hood is first placed over the print. Then some superglue is heated to about 120°F (60°C), so that it boils and the fumes waft over the print. Chemicals in the fumes stick to the molecules that form the print. This process not only makes the print more noticeable, but also provides a perfect surface for dust to stick to.

4. Examiners spend most of their time searching for prints on objects, but sometimes they need to take prints from dead bodies, either at the scene or during an autopsy. Getting prints from a dead body can be difficult. Rigor mortis, a stiffening of the muscles that occurs 2-6 hours after death, can cause the muscles of the hands to clench. After about 24 hours, the muscles relax and an expert can straighten the hand and get a set of prints. Taking prints from a body that has been in water for some time can be difficult as the deceased's skin often peels off. In this case, a technician may have to wrap the person's skin around his or her own finger to get a print.

crime scene. After all, no criminal deliberately leaves a full set of prints behind, so police often have to work with marks that are partially smudged or on surfaces that are too small to contain a whole print. There is no doubt that these new technologies will make solving crimes easier, but it is a matter of time before they are cost-effective and therefore widely used.

OUT WITH THE OLD

The next step in the technological assistance to crime fighting is, wherever possible, to do away with paper and cards altogether. A suspect called in for questioning places his fingers on a scanner pad, and the computer creates a digital image of the print, then uses specialized image analysis to search for identifying features. This image and the accompanying analysis can be stored in a computer, used to check against existing records, and sent to any police force in the world with the click of a mouse. It's this sort of electronic fingerprint that is being incorporated into some biometric security systems; paper records are on their way out.

Some are concerned, however, with the advent of computerized fingerprinting, that the palm database will not be as carefully maintained. Palm prints are as important identifiers as fingerprints, as they have eight to ten times more minutiae than fingerprints. Had it not been for the discovery of a palm print during the investigation of the murders of Margaret and Scott Benson in Florida in 1985, police would likely not have convicted their prime suspect in the case (see page 154). Palm-print scanners are being refined for common usage, but this technology is more difficult because of the many contours on the hand. The storage of a larger file is also a concern.

A dusted thumbprint is photographed with a scale for measurement.

Robert B. Kennedy

Forensic Identification Research Services, Ottawa, Canada

A typical day in FIRS (Forensic Identification Research Services) encompasses research in barefoot morphology, preparing for and giving lectures and courses relating to physical evidence, and preparing forensic evidence for court presentation.

9:00 A.M. I start my day by looking at the evidence taken from footprints taken from a recent crime scene. Forensic barefoot morphology is a method by which the weight-bearing areas of the bottom of a bare foot, excluding ridge detail, are compared to an impression left in some sort of medium (mud, blood, insole of a shoe, for example) found at a scene of a crime, for the purposes of excluding or linking suspects to the crime. Human beings can take thousands of steps a day, wearing footwear for many of those steps throughout a lifetime. As the foot generates heat and sweat, and puts pressure on the inside of the footwear, the footwear responds by stretching and molding to the foot. Areas of the insoles in the footwear become compressed and stained, such as the toe pads, ball area, and heel. These areas, as well as accidental characteristics that are made during wear (such as blister or callous formation) are compared and characterized during this forensic analysis.

9:30 A.M. On receiving any evidence from a crime scene, I initial and date all packages before opening them. My examination begins with barefoot impressions that were found in blood at the crime scene, which were photographed before they could be disturbed by a full search of the scene. I have these photographed using a scale so the impression can be photographically enlarged 1:1.

10:30 A.M. The investigating officers already have a suspect for this crime, and have taken ink impressions from his feet. The photographs I have for comparison with the bloody footprints are thorough, and include shots of the top, sides, and bottom of each bare foot from the suspect. These are also photographed using the same scale.

11:30 A.M. The evidence from the crime scene also includes the footwear the suspect was wearing at the time of arrest. This is cut apart and all debris, hair, fibers, and dirt are collected and packaged for possible further examination. The barefoot impressions found inside the footwear are also photographed.

1:30 P.M. I can now begin to look at all of the evidence in more detail. I compare the impressions from the crime scene to the shapes, placements, and contours of the barefoot impressions from the suspect, and conclude that he was at the scene of the crime. This does not immediately confirm his guilt, but does place him at the scene, and increases the likelihood that he committed the crime.

3:30 P.M. I begin to write a report, based on my findings, and stating my conclusions from the examination. All the evidence is then secured in case I am required to give testimony in a court of law about my findings.

CASE STUDY: Anatomy of Murder

VICTIM Dr. George Parkman
CAUSE OF DEATH Beating
WHERE Boston, Massachusetts, United States
WHEN November 23, 1849

The Crime

Boston's academic circles were shaken by a mysterious disappearance in the approach to the Thanksgiving holiday of November 1849. Dr. George Parkman, a professor of anatomy at Harvard's Medical College, had made the mistake of lending $438, a substantial sum of money at the time, to Dr. John Webster, Harvard professor of chemistry and mineralogy, and was having trouble recovering the money. On Friday, November 23, he went to Webster's office and laboratory to deliver the ultimatum that unless the money was repaid, Parkman would condemn him to social and professional ruin by making his debt public knowledge.

He never returned home. Webster admitted Parkman had called at his office but claimed that the debt had been repaid in full. He suggested that Parkman may have been attacked by thieves and murdered on his way home, and there was a supposed sighting of him at around 5:00 P.M. that same afternoon on the opposite side of the city.

The Case

Parkman was never seen alive again. Instead, his fate was revealed by a janitor at the Medical College named Ephraim Littlefield. On the day Parkman visited Webster and then disappeared, Littlefield had found the dividing wall with Webster's locked office was extremely hot to the touch. On the other side of the wall was an assay oven used for Webster's work, and when Littlefield asked why the wall was so hot, Webster said he had been conducting experiments. When Webster left his office, Littlefield set about breaking through the wall into the laboratory. On discovering a human pelvis and two parts of a leg, Littlefield called the police.

The Evidence

When the police searched the office, they found more human remains. The largest were parts of a human chest found in a storage box. A team of specialists measured the remains and confirmed that they belonged to a single victim, a male in his 50s who had been around 5 feet, 10 inches (178 cm) tall. This was a fairly close match to the missing Parkman, who was 5 feet, 11 inches (180 cm) tall and just 60 years old, but the final, crucial evidence was found in the ashes contained in the oven: a set of dentures that had survived the high temperatures. They were compared with the original mold kept by Parkman's dentist. The result was a perfect match and the remains were assumed to be those of the missing Parkman. Webster was arrested.

The Outcome

At Webster's trial, his lawyer tried to discredit the dental evidence by producing another set of dentures unrelated to the case, which also fitted Dr. Keep's mold. Webster's attempt to commit suicide by taking strychnine nevertheless suggested his guilt, and he was convicted and executed the summer after Parkman's disappearance. Just before he was hanged, Webster confessed to having beaten Parkman to death with a wooden club, after which he cut up his body.

CASE STUDY: A Mass Fingerprinting

VICTIM Julie Anne Devaney
CAUSE OF DEATH Blows to the head
WHERE Blackburn, Lancashire, United Kingdom
WHEN September 15, 1948

The Crime

In the Lancashire, U.K. town of Blackburn at 1:20 A.M. on September 15, 1948, the night nurse in one of the children's wards at Queen's Park Hospital was making her rounds when she noticed that one of her six charges, three-year-old Julie Anne Devaney, was missing. Next to the empty cot was a large glass laboratory bottle containing sterile water, but nothing else out of the ordinary. The police were called, and the hospital grounds were searched, where they found the little girl's body just an hour-and-a-half after the alarm was raised. She had been sexually assaulted and had suffered heavy blows to the head.

The Case

Finding the identity of the killer depended on the meager physical evidence left behind at the scene. In addition to the bottle of water, which carried several sets of fingerprints, there were faint traces of footprints in the highly waxed surface of the ward floor, which showed the killer had taken off his shoes to avoid making too much noise. Although there was nothing about the prints to unmask the killer, they did show he had walked to three of the cots before reaching that of Julie, and had picked up the bottle on the way. He had then placed it on the floor before picking her up and making his escape, so one set of fingerprints on the bottle was almost certainly his.

The Evidence

Police decided that only someone with local knowledge could have found a way into the ward and pick out the hiding place for the girl's body in the grounds in complete darkness. So they began the first mass-fingerprinting of the population on a truly heroic scale. First they compared the prints on the bottle with everyone with a legitimate reason to be in the ward at any time. These alone amounted to 642 people, but finally they eliminated all but one set of prints on the bottle, which had to be those of the killer. Next, they fingerprinted every male over the age of 16 who had been in the town on the night of the murder. After two months, more than 45,000 sets of prints had been taken and checked, but none were found to match those on the bottle.

The Outcome

The police had so far worked with identity cards, still in use after the war, and the electoral register. They moved on to use another wartime measure still in operation—the ration books that gave every citizen access to essential foods. When police checked the records of the issue of ration books in Blackburn against their fingerprint records, they found as many as 200 people had not been checked. Among the missing suspects was a 22-year-old man named Peter Griffiths, an ex-soldier now working in a local flour mill. His prints were the 46,253 set taken and were a perfect match for those on the bottle. His stockinged feet were the right size to match casts taken of the tracks found in the ward, and fibers from the girl's nightgown were found on his clothes. He was tried and convicted of murder, and went to the gallows almost six months to the day after the death of his victim.

CASE STUDY: Trail of a Serial Killer

VICTIMS 40 to 50 victims

CAUSE OF DEATH Various

WHERE Tallahassee and Pensacola, Florida, United States

WHEN 1969–1978

The Crime

Sometimes a killer may be smart enough, or lucky enough, to evade detection for several killings in succession. Ted Bundy was one of the most prolific American serial killers, carrying out a series of murders of young women over a nine-year period across a huge swath of the United States. He began killing in California in 1969, moved north into Oregon and Washington, and then headed east into Colorado and Utah. Surprisingly, he was identified on several occasions as present in the area where murders took place, but there was no specific evidence to prove his guilt. Even when he finally did make a mistake, and was jailed for the attempted murder of a young woman, he managed to escape and subsequently resumed his violent and grisly pattern.

The Case

Ted Bundy made the mistake that led to his first capture in November 1974, when he reached Salt Lake City. Pretending to be a plainclothes police officer, he ordered 18-year-old Carol DaRonch to get into his VW Beetle to go to the parking lot where someone had been seen trying to break into her automobile. He was believable enough at first, but when he tried to handcuff her and, when that failed, to hit her with a crowbar, she managed to escape. Police began watching for VW Beetles, although

these were extremely common on the roads of the United States. Finally, on August 16, 1975, a Salt Lake City police officer pulled over a Beetle to check the driver's papers. Inside was Ted Bundy, with crowbar and handcuffs. He was tried and sentenced to 15 years in jail for attempted murder.

Meanwhile, police were collecting more and more evidence from earlier murders that pointed in Bundy's direction. But before additional charges could be brought in the summer of 1977, he had escaped custody and been recaptured, only to escape again six months later. This time he moved to Florida and the killings began again.

On one evening in January 1978, Bundy attacked five women on the Tallahassee campus of Florida State University, leaving two dead, two seriously injured by vicious head blows, and another well enough to identify him. He was finally recaptured in Pensacola after he had killed one final victim, a 12-year-old girl named Kimberly Leach.

The Evidence

By the time Leach's body was found it had decomposed too badly to provide much direct evidence, although bloodstains and semen traces on her underwear were of the same type as Bundy's and prints identical to the soles of his shoes were found next to the body. But the evidence that had most effect on the jury at his trial would be a series of bite marks on the breast and buttocks of one of his Tallahassee victims, Lisa Levy. Odontologist Dr. Lowell J. Levine showed the jury photographs of Bundy's teeth and compared the unusual features with the bite marks, to convince it that the match was a perfect one.

The Outcome

Ted Bundy's trial for the Florida State University murders began on June 25, 1979, in Miami. On July 23, he was found guilty of both killings and sentenced a week later to the electric chair. He was also charged with the murder of Kimberly Leach early the following year, and was again given a death sentence. A series of appeals over 10 years proved unsuccessful, and Bundy was executed on January 24, 1989, at Raiford State Penitentiary, having confessed beforehand to as many as 40 murders.

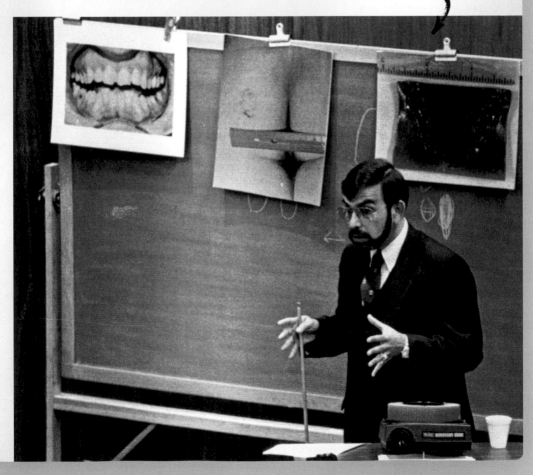

Dr. Levine, a forensic odontologist, testifies at Bundy's trial that the bite marks found on the buttock of victim Lisa Levy reflect characteristics of Bundy's teeth.

CASE STUDY: The Jagged Tooth

VICTIM Linda Peacock
CAUSE OF DEATH Strangulation
WHERE Biggar, South Lanarkshire, Scotland
WHEN August 6, 1967

The Crime

On August 6, 1967, 15-year-old Linda Peacock went missing from her home in a small Scottish town some 25 miles (40 km) southwest of Edinburgh. At around 10:00 P.M. on the night of her disappearance, witnesses had seen a girl matching her description standing by the cemetery gates in town talking to a young man, and another witness reported hearing a scream around 20 minutes later. Early the following morning, her body was found inside the churchyard. She had been beaten and strangled with a rope.

The Case

When her body was examined, it was clear her killer had not raped her, although her clothes were disturbed and there was a prominent oval bruise on her right breast. Closer inspection showed this was a bite mark, which was photographed. Because there were unusual features about the bite, investigators decided to call in forensic dentistry expert Dr. Warren Harvey, who confirmed that specific characteristics of the mark could help identify the killer.

The Evidence

The police had checked almost the whole population of the small town and the surrounding area, a total of more than 3,000 people, with no success at all. The only group of people left unchecked was the 29 inmates of a juvenile detention center in the town, and Dr. Harvey decided this was a small enough group to make dental comparisons viable. The key feature of the bite mark was one unusually jagged tooth. All the inmates had been asked to provide a bite impression for comparison purposes. There were five where the resemblance to the bite on Linda's body was close enough to cause suspicion. One in particular was 17-year-old Gordon Hay, who was serving time in the center for breaking into a factory. He had told other inmates the night before her disappearance that he had met Linda at the local fair, and that he wanted to have sex with her. He was reported missing on the night she vanished and was seen on his return to be out of breath, disheveled, and covered in mud.

The Outcome

Unmasking Hay as the killer depended on producing a more exact match between his teeth and the bite mark. Dr. Harvey took a more precise impression and noticed evidence of sharp-edged pits in the tips of the upper and lower right canine teeth, the result of a rare condition called hypocalcination. This in itself was highly unusual. In Hay's case, the pit in the upper tooth was lower than that in the lower canine, which when combined with the site of the pits made a perfect match with the bite mark. To back up the diagnosis, Dr. Harvey examined the teeth of 342 young soldiers of similar age to Hay, and found two with pitted teeth, one of whom had a pit and hypocalcination. None had two pits and hypocalcination. Though the defense lawyers tried to discredit the dental evidence, when considered with the witness statements on his absence the night of the girl's murder and his condition on his return, it was enough to result in a guilty verdict.

CASE STUDY: The Killing of Kevin Jackson

VICTIM	Kevin Jackson
CAUSE OF DEATH	Stab wound
WHERE	Bradford, West Yorkshire, England
WHEN	December 30, 2001

The Crime

On December 30, 2001, 31-year-old Kevin Jackson was stabbed in the head while trying to prevent thieves stealing his father's automobile from his home in Yorkshire. He died two days later, on New Year's Day, leaving a wife and two young sons. It was an event that shocked not only the local community, but the nation as a whole, and police were determined to solve the case as quickly as possible. The victim's stab wounds became the focus of their investigation, as they were not consistent with those made by a knife, but had been inflicted using some kind of tool—the same tool that had been used to break into the vehicle.

The Case

British police used hardware specialists to help them identify the kind of tool used. The specialists started with the marks made by the tool in the lock of the automobile. Because no two tools are alike, they do not leave identical impressions. Obvious differences such as size, width, and shape are things that set tools apart, but there are also other, minute, differences that can be discovered when examining a tool in the laboratory using microscopic equipment. These might include marks left on a tool through its use, or during the manufacturing, finishing, or grinding processes.

The Evidence

The specialists' reports led to one suspect and, on arresting 21-year-old Rashad Zaman a few days later, they found a screwdriver in the back of his automobile, which was identified as the tool that had made the incriminating marks. Furthermore, microscopic traces of blood inside joints of the handle matched Jackson's blood. Even if DNA testing had proved inconclusive when matching the blood found on the screwdriver in this case, the tool was a positive link to the automobile.

These weren't the only impressions that yielded important evidence, however. The police also arrested two other suspects, 20-year-old Rangzaib Akhtar and 21-year-old Raees Khan. Among the items they took from their homes was a pair of boots, which turned out to be spattered with blood that matched Kevin Jackson's DNA profile. Shoeprints at the crime scene matched the boots, and inside the boots police found skin flakes that matched Zaman's DNA profile and hairs that matched Khan. Police concluded that the boots probably belonged to Khan but had been worn occasionally by Zaman. Another set of shoeprints left in the snow at the scene matched a pair of Nike sneakers later found at Akhtar's house.

The Outcome

A final piece of evidence in this case came from skin scrapings found under the dead man's nails. When a DNA profile was obtained from the skin scrapings, and run through the National DNA Database, it was found to match Khan. In December 2002—just a year after the attack—each of the three suspects received a life sentence for murder at Leeds Crown Court.

CASE STUDY: A Matter of Inheritance

VICTIMS Margaret and Scott Benson

CAUSE OF DEATH Automobile bomb

WHERE Naples, Florida, United States

WHEN July 9, 1985

The Crime

The Benson family lived in Naples, in the southern part of Florida, enjoying an enviable lifestyle based on the profits made from Lancaster Leaf, a tobacco company founded by the father of Margaret Benson. But all was not well with the Benson family, and Margaret had become increasingly worried about the behavior of her 35-year-old son Steven, who had a string of failed and expensive business ventures behind him. She was already convinced he had started to steal money from her, and she feared his desperate need for funds might lead to more violent action. In the summer of 1985, she asked the family lawyer to investigate Steven's affairs. Within days, she and her adopted son Scott, 21, had been blown to pieces while sitting in the family station wagon outside their house.

Steven Benson on trial for the murder of his mother and adoptive brother, in a bid to benefit from a $10 million inheritance.

The Case

The facts seemed straightforward enough. Steven Benson was marking out a site for a new home, and had driven the 1978 Chevrolet Suburban to his grandmother's house to pick up the materials he needed. He stopped at a local store for coffee and rolls, which he took back to the family house for breakfast. At 9:00 A.M. his mother, brother, and his sister Carol Lynn were in the automobile ready to travel out to the site with him. Steven said he had left his tape measure in the house, and went to fetch it. He threw the ignition keys to Scott and told him he could start up the vehicle for the drive. As Steven walked into the house, Scott turned the ignition key and the vehicle exploded with enormous force. Margaret and Scott were killed instantly. Carol Lynn survived, though she was severely injured.

The Evidence

Steven's apparent lack of concern at the violent deaths of his mother and adopted brother, not to mention the serious injuries to his sister, triggered deep suspicion on the part of the investigators. Could he have devised some kind of explosive device to wreck the automobile, kill his family, and leave him as the sole inheritor of a multi-million-dollar fortune? After a painstaking search of the wreckage of the vehicle, they found fragments of galvanized metal pipe that had been used as the bomb casing. The ends of the pipe had been sealed by a pair of threaded end caps, both of which were intact, and their markings showed that one had been made by a company called Grinnell, the other by Union Brand. Also found in the wreckage were four small 1.5-volt batteries, a switch, and a fragment of circuit board which did not belong in the car's electrical system.

Teams of detectives toured local hardware stores, scrap yards, and building sites to check where the pipe and end caps had come from. Finally, they found a store where records showed a pair of threaded end caps had been bought just four days before the killings, and the assistant who dealt with the sale thought he remembered a man matching Steven Benson's description. The sales documentation was treated for fingerprints, and one of them showed a clear palm print, which proved to be that of Steven Benson.

The Outcome

On August 21, 1985, Steven Benson was arrested for the murder of his mother and brother. Financial records showed he had indeed been stealing from his mother. Benson was worried she would discover what was going on, and disinherit him from his share of the family wealth as a result. He was tried the following year. The defense tried to pin responsibility on Scott, who it emerged was the illegitimate son of Carol Lynn but adopted by her mother. The jury still found Steven guilty of both killings.

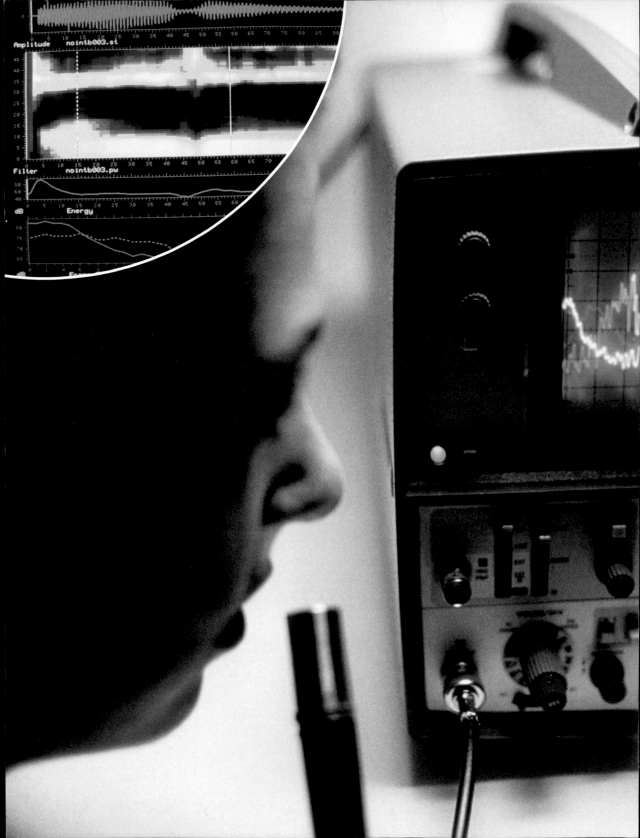

Amplitude   nointb003.st

45
40
35
30
25
20
15
10
5

Filter   nointb003.pw

80
60

dB   Energy

80
75
70

8

IN WRITING AND ON THE RECORD

Handwriting experts can trace documents to their writers just as criminologists can identify potential suspects by their fingerprints. Each individual has a particular way of writing—the size and shape of the letters, whether or not words slope on the page—a trademark style that belongs to that person alone. The same is true for an individual's voice, which is unique in terms of pitch, tone, pace, and dialect. Forensic advances and computer analysis have made it increasingly difficult for criminals to disguise their voices in order to avoid being identified.

CASE STUDIES:
- Voiceprint Betrayal
- The Letter Giveaway
- Written in Blood
- Deferred Justice
- Cell Phone Capture

The Paper Trail

Documents can be extremely useful in resolving a crime. Whether handwritten or printed by machine, or a combination of both, a document has a story to tell that can be uncovered by an expert.

A forensic handwriting expert compares two handwriting samples side by side.

WHAT'S IN A DOCUMENT?

A document may be a ticket showing the time that a person crossed a toll bridge. In one situation this could corroborate a suspect's alibi, while in another it could indicate that he was near a crime scene at the relevant time. A document examiner needs to consider whether there is any evidence that the document had been forged or altered, and who had created any handwriting on it, such as a signature.

SLEIGHT OF HAND

From the moment a child picks up a pencil and starts scribbling, he or she will begin to develop a unique way of holding and moving the pencil. With age, this turns into a unique handwriting style. We are, after all, used to being able to recognize who has sent us a letter just from the handwriting on the envelope, and you can remember these individual styles even when you only receive mail from someone once a year—such as the aunt who sends you a birthday card.

Handwriting experts take this widespread ability much further. They can analyze a set of examples that they know were written by

one particular person, and then assess whether the same author penned the text in a questioned document. The expert looks for uniquely identifying features, such as:
- Variations in the slope of letters
- Spacing between letters
- Spacing between words
- Indentations on the paper that show how hard the person pressed
- Relative differences in letter heights
- Where each letter begins and finishes

Assume the police have found a letter and want evidence that a particular person wrote it. If they find a writing pad or notebook of similar paper in a suspect's house, they may have the evidence they need. When you write on one sheet of a pad, the pen often indents the sheet below. These indentations may be too slight for anyone to make sense of just by looking at them. But sprinkle fine particles of printer toner on it, place a plastic sheet on top, and then wave an electrostatic wand over it, and the toner will gather in the indentations. In one simple move you can go from a blank sheet to compelling evidence.

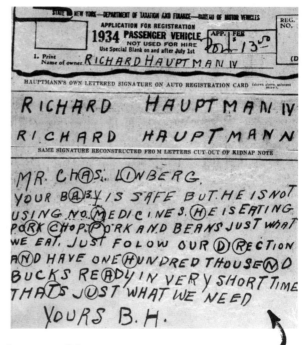

Signatures are obvious targets for forgers. The forger either traces the outline of a signature onto a document, fills it in with ink, and then rubs out the tracing marks, or uses a light box to make the original signature visible on the new document and draws over that. A big giveaway is that these signatures can often look more labored than the original version.

Also, if more than one signature is needed on a set of documents, then an expert may notice they're all absolutely identical—something that is more unlikely to happen if the signatures are genuine.

Two documents from the Lindbergh kidnapping case, in which letters from a ransom note are compared to those from a signature of suspect Richard Hauptmann. The two share a number of common characteristics.

Masters of Disguise

Some criminals try to disguise their handwriting to avoid revealing their identity. Some change the size of the letters and their slant, write in another person's handwriting style, or deliberately misspell words. Others may print in block capitals or write with their other hand.

As part of their work, handwriting experts must collect the right sort of "exemplar" samples—samples of writing that the forensic document examiner can use to check a person's normal style. These samples need to be written using the same sort of pencil or pen as had been used in the original evidence, and on the same sort of paper.

On occasion, documents such as letters to banks, employers, or friends can be admitted as examples of a person's normal writing. The problem here is that, on the whole, no one has witnessed these letters being written, so the prosecution could have problems when it comes to presenting these as evidence if the case comes before a court. The way around this is to get the suspect to produce a piece of writing in front of witnesses. If the suspect is guilty, he or she may want to disguise their writing. To counter this possibility, the person is seated at a comfortable desk and has the original text dictated to them on three separate occasions. Each time the original is kept out of sight, as is any previous version. The person who is dictating gives no indication of spelling or punctuation. Unless the person is very practiced, it will be difficult regularly to reproduce specific spelling errors, or features within the writing that break from the suspect's normal style. An expert may not be able to say what the person's true style is, but may come to the conclusion that the suspect has something to hide.

PRINTERS' MARKS

Typewriters and computer-linked printers give an initial impression of producing a very uniform script. But there is plenty of irregularity for a forensic expert to work on.

1. Few people still use typewriters, but some documents that are important for forensic examinations are many years old and were created with these machines. Anyone wanting to alter such documents will need to use one, or try to imitate its text by hand. A document examiner must therefore have a good understanding of outdated printing methods.

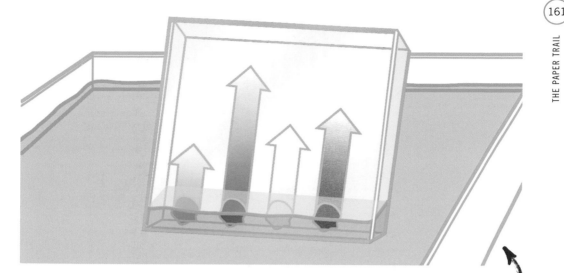

2. Any machine that uses keys to strike a character onto the paper is bound to have anomalies in one or more of its letters. An "o" may be partially filled in, or an "l" may have a partial break somewhere in the character. Checking two or more documents with a microscope could establish that they have come from the same machine.

3. Alternatively, looking at all the text in a single document may reveal that one word or numeral has been added by a different machine. A word like "not" could change a document's entire meaning; an added zero or two could alter the value of a bank check significantly, and evidence that a name has been erased can be detected under infrared light.

4. Documents from laser and jet printers leave their mark in features such as the unique way the roller leaves indentations on the paper. Looking through a microscope at the way in which toner binds to the fibers in a sheet of paper gives vital clues about the type of printer used, and using chromatography to break down the pigments can indicate what make of toner was in the printer. With experience, an expert can estimate the age of a document by assessing how much of the solvent used to carry the inks to the paper is present in the writing.

There are many methods used to analyze inks, such as thin-layer chromatography, which separates substances by the speed at which they move up a plate covered with silica gel.

SHINE A LIGHT

Whether a document is created by hand or by machine, analyzing the ink could show that the writing was created using two different makes of pigment. This would immediately raise suspicions that the original document had been altered in some way.

The overall impression in natural light may be that all of the ink used in a document is the same color. A simple way to spot differences in ink is to take the document and shine a light source on it that consists of a very narrow band of wavelengths, such as infrared or ultraviolet light. Under such light sources, letters written with different ink to the main part of the document stand out in a different color to the rest, because pigments in the inks reflect different wavelengths. One crude test that is easy to perform is to hold a document under a yellow streetlight. The sodium bulbs create monochromatic light and can sometimes reveal if different inks are present on the same page.

On occasion, someone may have deliberately drawn over part of a document to hide the writing. Here handwriting experts use infrared light, which can penetrate the top layer of ink, and infrared-sensitive film, which may be able to detect anything written underneath. The technique will work only if the crossing out was done in a type of ink that is significantly different to that used in creating the original text. Infrared light and photography can also help decipher charred documents by increasing the contrast between the ink and the burned paper, and thus restoring the text.

FAKING IT

Forgers are becoming increasingly skilled at using high-quality scanners, software, and computer printers to create fake documents. The possibilities run from counterfeit currency to false passports and forged bank bonds. This same computing power can, however, be turned to good use by forensic image experts in an effort to spot those forgeries. Using a scanner, a document examiner grabs a digitized image of a suspect document and feeds this information into a computer. Using image-analysis software, the expert alters the image's contrasts and colors. This shows up any anomalies that could indicate forgery.

Valuable documents often contain markings printed in inks that show up only when specific wavelengths of light are shone on them. The frequencies used are normally not present in normal daylight, but a scanner that can shine ultraviolet light on a document may be able to detect the hidden security features on genuine documents.

Hearing Voices

The basic idea behind voice analysis is simple. Just as everyone has a unique fingerprint, they also have a unique voiceprint.

By this, investigators mean that you can analyze the way that a person produces words to the extent that you can pinpoint who is speaking.

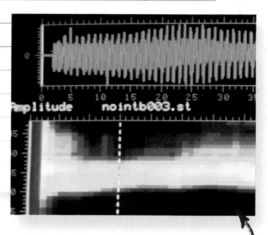

Computer graphics show a voiceprint of the word "baby."

TELEPHONE GIVEAWAY

Voice analysis is increasingly being used in situations where investigators are attempting to track down a person who has made repeated malicious, threatening, or obscene telephone calls. It can also provide useful leads when there are recordings of 911 calls made from the scene of a crime while a crime is taking place. Some recordings pick up words not only from the victim but also from the assailants.

Although there is some debate about how accurate any voiceprint assessment can be, plenty of court cases have turned on the basis of voiceprint evidence.

On top of this, voiceprint analysis has helped investigators on the (relatively rare) occasions when a murderer has telephoned the police to let them know the location of a body, or when, in the case of a hit-and-run accident, a person calls for an ambulance to attend the victim. In the case of the suspected killer of Neil LaFeve in Wisconsin in 1971, it was the voice of the suspect's grandmother that gave the game away (see page 167).

Sound Values

A person generates words by creating vibrations in the air. These are shaped by the tension that he or she applies to the vocal cords in the throat, as well as how the muscles in the tongue and jaw contract and alter the shape of the space inside their mouth. The resulting sound is also influenced by the shape of anatomical features like the sinuses and the air passages in the nose.

As this anatomy varies considerably between people, there is a natural variation in people's voices. Add to this the effect of education, social upbringing, national and regional environment, and age, and you have a huge number of variables that makes each person's voice distinct.

A GOOD EAR

A light spectrograph splits a beam of light into the individual wave bands and then measures the intensity of each. A sound spectrograph splits a sound recording into different wavelengths and records the intensity of each. But with a sound spectrograph there is an added dimension—time. To make any sense of the complexities of speech, the sound spectrograph needs to record how the intensities of each wavelength of sound change over time. The result is a multicolored chart that streams out as sound information is played. The horizontal axis of a voiceprint represents time, the vertical axis shows the frequency, and the degree of darkness within each region of the graph indicates the intensity of that frequency.

As is the case in working with handwriting, a forensic expert needs an authentic example to compare with a crime-related one. In voice analysis, the reference example takes the form of a tape recording of the person's voice as he or she speaks normally. The expert notes any differences between this and the crime-related tape, and works out if the two samples were made by the same person.

In addition to using the spectrograph, forensic experts who work in voice analysis learn to listen intently. We all know how easy it is to recognize the voice of people we know when they call us on the telephone. Very often the caller doesn't even need to announce their name before we know who they are. Voiceprint experts look to build on this type of unthinking skill. The sorts of things voice analysts listen to are breath patterns, inflections, unusual speech habits, and accents. They compare single sounds, as well as series of sounds, for similarities and discrepancies.

MATCH PERFECT

Although voice analysis has been going on for more than a century, and voiceprints have been used in several cases in the United States and United Kingdom to confirm the identity of telephone callers, forensic voice experts still debate quite how reliable the tests are. Voice analysts need to be well trained before they have a chance of persuading a judge and jury that their evidence is valid.

All the same, there's a growing consensus that if you find at least 20 key speech sounds that appear to be identical between a piece of taped voice evidence and a reference recording you can conclude that they match. Furthermore, the American Board of Recorded Evidence says that finding 15 matching sounds and no unexplained differences can be taken as a probable identification, while 10 sounds with no unexplained differences gives a possible identification.

Voiceprint techniques can also be used to eliminate people from suspicion. Ten or more differences mean that the voice on the evidence tape is possibly not the person under suspicion; 15 or more nonmatching sounds mean that they are probably not matched and 20 indicate that the two tapes come from different people.

The Grandaddy of Voice Analysis

In 1882, Alexander Melville Bell published a book called *Visible Speech*, in which he showed a way of visually representing voice patterns. His method was limited to assessing the way people use punctuation, but he showed that even with this small part of the spoken word, he could distinguish different people. His son, Alexander Graham Bell, took the idea further. Initially motivated by the desire to help deaf people, he ended up using his inventions to develop the first telephones. Over half a century later, in 1941, the Bell Laboratories in New Jersey produced a sound spectrograph that could map a voice onto paper, and slowly forensic scientists realized that they had a new weapon in their armory. Voiceprints were first used in criminal investigations in the early 1960s, by New York City police who were investigating bomb threats by telephone to major airlines. The technology took over two years to perfect and it was even longer before such evidence was admissible in court. Today when voiceprints are used as evidence, certain precautions are observed to make sure it is given in the right context and properly understood by juries.

Nicola Aranyi

Principal Analyst, Lincolnshire Police, United Kingdom

Being a criminal intelligence analyst is all about having the ability to look at a problem from a wide angle, and being able to put the pieces of the puzzle together to make recommendations and inferences that will aid crime prevention or further an investigation.

criminal intelligence analyst

9:00 A.M. I begin my day by looking at the crimes recorded over the previous 24 hours, using a computer database that logs crime reports from a variety of sources, including the public and police officers. Often I am given set priorities for the types of crime that need attention, and I work on my own initiative within those guidelines, assessing if any particular crime trends or hot spots are emerging and mapping them with specialized computer software.

10:30 A.M. I have been asked to work on a particular burglary. I analyze the modus operandi (MO), study the intelligence picture—who is out of prison, who lives in the area, what information has been received from informants—and set out to provide a total picture for senior officers in the department.

11:45 A.M. On reading the notes from this case I am reminded of a similar case two months back, in the same part of town. The MO was the same each time: the offender broke in through a back door using a garden fork or shovel and stole electronic equipment. As an ongoing task, I had been mapping the crime picture for this prior case, monitoring all the intelligence, which centered on a group of teenagers who were suspected of committing up to 200 local burglaries. I ascertained which crimes had produced trace evidence and advised the fingerprint criminalists to run checks.

1:15 P.M. I begin to compile all the necessary evidence to present to detectives investigating the crimes, who can then use it to plan a surveillance operation. I assemble charts that show sequences of events, criminal networks, and lifestyle patterns, such as known associates of the suspects, their homes, the cars they drove, and who handled the property. There is enough evidence here for the police to carry the work forward and make arrests.

2:00 P.M. A new case has just been brought to my attention—the rape of a young woman. I begin by collating the movements of the victim on charts and maps; analyzing information from the witness statements, security cameras, and other intelligence sources to reconstruct what took place. There are several messages on the victim's cell phone, which may be used to carry out some voiceprint analysis and could lead to a possible suspect.

2:30 P.M. I brief a colleague to look for possible suspects in the case.

4:45 P.M. My colleague and I compare our results. Once these have been charted, any gaps in intelligence become apparent, indicating where further investigation should be focused. As the case progresses, I expect to receive intelligence updates from the investigators, so that I can add more detail to the overall picture that should, eventually, assist in the apprehension of the offender.

CASE STUDY: Voiceprint Betrayal

VICTIM Neil LaFeve

CAUSE OF DEATH Rifle wounds and decapitation

WHERE Brown County, Wisconsin, United States

WHEN September 24, 1971

The Crime

Neil LaFeve had been posting signs in the Sensiba Wildlife Area in Brown County, Wisconsin, when he was shot repeatedly in the head with a .22 caliber rifle and then decapitated. Police found his body on September 24, 1971, following an extended search of the Wisconsin woods where he worked as a game warden. A couple of .22 caliber shells were found in the immediate vicinity, and it looked as if an attempt had been made to bury some of the victim's remains. September 23 had been LaFeve's 32nd birthday, and his wife had reported him missing when he failed to return home for a party she had been arranging.

The Case

Investigators suspected that the assailant might have been a local poacher bearing some kind of grudge against the game warden—LaFeve was known for taking a firm line with anyone seen breaking the law. The police started interviewing people who LaFeve had caught in the recent past. Among them was a 21-year-old, Brian Hussong, who had been caught shooting pheasants out of season earlier in the year. He soon became the police investigators' chief suspect when, out of all potential suspects, he was the only one who refused to take a polygraph test.

The Evidence

Toward the end of a three-month investigation, the police got the breakthrough they needed. Under the United States Electronic Surveillance Law, investigating officers had managed to get permission to tap Brian Hussong's telephone—the first time in the state of Wisconsin that such a measure had been undertaken in a murder case. With the police listening to the call, the suspect telephoned his grandmother asking her to hide his guns and then to provide him with an alibi for the time of the crime. During their conversation Agnes Hussong seemed happy to cooperate, but police were soon on her doorstep to recover Hussong's .22 caliber rifle. Just nine days after tapping the suspect's phone, the investigating officers were able to arrest him for the murder of Neil LaFeve.

The Outcome

When the case came to court, it was Hussong's grandmother, Agnes, who became the focus of attention for the prosecution. She denied having had the telephone conversation with her grandson, in which she said would hide the gun. However, voice experts from the Michigan Voice Identification Unit proved that the voice in the taped phone call did belong to her, by matching it with another recording of her voice and comparing them on spectrograph. The evidence was enough to convict Hussong and it was not long before he was serving a life sentence in prison. Ten years after his arrest, Hussong managed to escape from prison and was shot dead by a posse of U.S. deputies, who had been sent after him.

CASE STUDY: The Letter Giveaway

VICTIM Dr. Herman Tarnower
CAUSE OF DEATH Gunshot wounds
WHERE Westchester County, New York, United States
WHEN March 10, 1980

The Crime

On March 10, 1980, Jean Harris drove to the home of her lover, Dr. Herman Tarnower in Westchester County, New York, taking with her a .32-caliber revolver. Arriving at 10.00 P.M., she found him asleep in bed. She woke him up and they argued heatedly. During the course of their fight, Tarnower was shot four times, fatally.

The Case

Harris and Tarnower had been lovers for 14 years but, by early 1980, he was beginning to tire of her.

Aged 69, the renowned cardiologist had developed the Scarsdale Diet, and Harris was the 57-year-old headmistress of a prestigious girls' preparatory school. She suffered from depression and was racked with self doubt about her relationship with Tarnower because of her age. She knew, for example, that he was in a long-term relationship with a younger

Jean Harris claimed she had planned to commit suicide and wished to see Tarnower one last time.

woman, Lynne Tryforos, a receptionist and medical assistant at the Scarsdale Clinic.

The Evidence

Matters came to a head when Tarnower invited both women to a banquet in his honor. Harris felt slighted and wrote him a long, caustic letter, in which she called Tryforos a slut, accused her of damaging clothes Harris had left at Tarnower's home, and called her a "vicious, adulterous psychotic." She sent the letter to Tarnower the day before he died.

The Outcome

At her trial, Harris's defense claimed that she had intended to shoot herself and that Tarnower's death had been a tragic accident, when things got out of hand during their heated argument. They referred to her bouts of depression and called numerous character witnesses on her behalf. Harris, however, appeared to show no remorse for what had occurred, and her description of events at Tarnower's home lacked conviction. She appeared at times depressed and at others agitated.

The ballistics evidence from the trial proved to be ambiguous. While the prosecution showed how the victim's wounds suggested he had been shot ruthlessly at point blank range, the defense used blood spatter patterns to prove that there had definitely been a struggle. A stalemate ensued until the prosecution introduced Harris's letter, the wording of which and the vicious nature of the attacks made against Tarnower and Tryforos proved enough to debunk the defense claim that Harris was a respectable woman who could not have deliberately murdered her lover. Harris was convicted of second-degree murder and sentenced to 15 years to life.

CASE STUDY: Written in Blood

VICTIM Ghislaine Marchal
CAUSE OF DEATH Stab wounds and beating
WHERE Mougins, France
WHEN June 23, 1991

The Crime

When the wealthy 65-year-old widow Ghislaine Marchal was found stabbed and beaten to death in the basement of her villa near Cannes, France, on June 23, 1991, the clues were easy to find.

The Case

While dying from her wounds, she had written on the wall in her own blood the damning words *"Omar m'a tuer…"*—French for "Omar has killed me." Her gardener, a Moroccan man named Omar Raddad, had disappeared, taking with him 4,000 francs ($800) believed to be in the house at the time. He did not remain at large for long and, once captured, was charged with Madame Marchal's murder and put on trial on January 24, 1992. He claimed that, at the time she was supposed to have been murdered, he had been sent on an errand to Cannes. Still, he was found guilty and sentenced to 18 years in prison.

The Evidence

Doubts began to surface. A graphologist claimed that the bloody message was in her writing, but would she really have mistakenly used the infinitive form of the verb *tuer*, meaning "to kill," rendering the message almost meaningless? She would almost certainly have used the word *tuée* or "killed," as a matter of instinct and basic grammar, even at such

a desperate moment. The defense brought in two other graphologists who claimed there were clear differences between the writing on the wall and Madame Marchal's hand.

She had been found dead in the basement, behind a door barricaded from the inside by an iron bar and an iron bedstead. Her hand was covered in blood, but detectives doubted anyone so grievously wounded could have written any message at all. Other contradictions continued to blur the picture: a pair of bloodstained gloves found in the kitchen sink had been burned in the fireplace, together with Madame Marchal's diary; there was no trace of blood on the clothing Raddad was wearing at the time; and DNA tests on the blood in the basement showed it was a mixture of Madame Marchal's blood and that of an unknown male, but definitely not Raddad. Finally, Professor Fournier, an expert in forensic medicine, was convinced that the murder had actually been carried out on the same day as the discovery of the body, a day later than claimed at the trial. If this was the case, Omar Raddad had an iron-clad alibi, having spent the day with relatives and friends.

The Outcome

Increasing doubts, and the efforts of Raddad's defense team, resulted in a partial presidential pardon in 1998. Having served four years of his sentence, Omar Raddad was released on September 4, and started work in a halal butcher's shop in Marseilles 10 days later. But, so far, his campaign for a retrial to reverse what he insists is a miscarriage of justice has been unsuccessful. The prosecution still insists that he killed his employer to steal money to pay off gambling debts, but the defense says he is merely a scapegoat for family members trying to steal from their wealthy relative.

CASE STUDY: Deferred Justice

VICTIMS Richard Phillips and Milton Curtis

CAUSE OF DEATH Gunshot wounds

WHERE El Segundo, California, United States

WHEN July 21, 1957

The Crime

Four teenagers in a vehicle in a lovers' lane in the suburb of Hawthorne were robbed by an armed stranger who appeared out of the darkness and took watches and money before tying them up and driving to a more secluded location. There he raped one of the girls and ordered all four out of the automobile before driving off. Later, two police officers, Richard Phillips and Milton Curtis, spotted a vehicle running a red light at a junction in El Segundo, 5 miles (3 km) from the crime scene. They flagged it down and wrote out a ticket, but the driver shot them both down. Though dying from his wounds, Phillips hit his attacker and the automobile with return fire. Both officers were found dead at the scene, and the stolen vehicle was later found abandoned in nearby Manhattan Beach.

The Case

The only clue was a pair of partial thumbprints left by the killer on the steering wheel of the abandoned vehicle, but there was no way to combine the prints to reconstruct a full print, and no national database to search for a match. Only when the murder weapon turned up in a garden in Manhattan Beach three years later, together with watches belonging to the teenagers, did a positive lead emerge. Ballistics checks confirmed the gun had been used to kill the police officers, and its serial number revealed it had

been bought from a gun store in Shreveport, Louisiana, by a George Wilson, just four days before the shootings. Further checks showed the name and the address given when buying the gun were both false, but the suspect had stayed at a local YMCA, and his handwriting was on the registration form.

The Evidence

Once again the trail went cold. Decades later, in 2002, detectives decided to use computer technology to recreate the thumbprint and enter it into the AFIS (Automated Fingerprint Identification System) national database. At last the owner of the print was identified as Gerald Mason, who had served a sentence the year before the murders for robbery and forgery. The records showed he was now living in Columbia, South Carolina.

Knowing who the suspect was gave the police an additional, and vital, piece of evidence—his handwritten application for a driving licence dating from 1959. When this was compared by handwriting experts with the George Wilson YMCA registration form, a series of matches in the width, height, and angle of each of the letters showed they had both been written by the same person.

The Outcome

In January 2003, Gerald Mason was charged with two murders, one rape, five charges of kidnapping, and four of robbery. When arrested, Mason broke down and wept. He was examined and found to have scars on his back from Phillips's bullet. Additional handwriting samples confirmed the experts' initial judgment. On March 24, 2003, he made a full confession on all charges, after which he was given two life sentences for the murders.

CASE STUDY: Cell Phone Capture

VICTIM Sidney Reso
CAUSE OF DEATH Heart attack
WHERE Morris Township, New Jersey, United States
WHEN April 29, 1992

Environmentalists were discounted, and the case was seen as straightforward extortion. Delivery of the ransom was agreed for June 18, with the FBI and police keeping watch. A man and woman were seen using pay phones that were identified as the sources of calls to the cell phone.

The Crime

On April 29, 1992, Sidney Reso, president of Exxon International, was kidnapped as he left his home in New Jersey. A ransom note instructed the company to arrange a cell phone account to receive further instructions. The kidnappers claimed to be environmental activists with a grudge against Exxon.

The Case

The culprits had made a mistake, however, because calls to cell phones can be traced.

A surveillance operation was mounted, concentrating on local pay phones. A man and woman made calls to the cell phone and delivered more notes, demanding $18.5 million, but the police and FBI were unable to catch them.

The Outcome

One of the criminals was spotted driving a rental vehicle, but was then lost. Eventually, the couple was arrested when they attempted to return the vehicle to the rental office. The suspects were Arthur and Jackie Seale. Arthur, a former policeman, had worked for Exxon as a security officer and had seen kidnapping Reso as an easy way of obtaining enough money to pay off substantial business debts. A week later, Jackie led police to where Reso was buried. The couple had never intended to murder him, but he had died from a heart attack as a result of their treatment. Arthur Seale pleaded guilty to murder, kidnapping, and extortion, receiving a life sentence; his wife Jackie was given 20 years for extortion.

The Evidence

An FBI profiler was called in to study the evidence and concluded from the phraseology of the notes that the writer had a security background and some connection to Reso or Exxon. The way in which Reso had been snatched suggested careful planning, but the reliance on a cell phone indicated inexperience in this kind of crime.

A photograph of Arthur Seale, taken on the day of the couple's arrest, June 18, 1992.

Glossary

Acquittal to be released from custody when found not guilty of a crime.

Alibi a defense, given by the accused, that he was elsewhere when a crime was committed.

Amphetamines a group of drugs used medically to combat fatigue and illicitly as a stimulant.

Antibody a molecule produced to fend off infections.

Arson deliberately setting property on fire.

Automatic weapon a firearm that uses the explosive force of one round of ammunition to mechanically load the next round and readies the gun to fire again.

Autopsy an examination of a human body that attempts to determine how the person died.

Ballistics the scientific study of how bullets and other projectiles travel through the air.

Blood spatter patterns characteristic shapes of blood marks that give information about how the blood was shed.

Chain of custody a record of who has examined a piece of forensic evidence from the moment that it was discovered.

Chloroform a solvent that is used to dissolve many materials that can't be dissolved in water.

Chromatography a range of techniques that break down chemical samples into their constituent parts.

Circumstantial (class) physical evidence category of evidence that can be used to infer particulars of an event but is not inherently objective.

CODIS Combined DNA Index System; used by the FBI to store genetic fingerprints.

Comparison microscope two microscopes coupled together so that the scientist can compare two samples simultaneously.

Cyanoacrylic the chemical in a group of glues that bind firmly to the amino acids, fatty acids, and proteins found in fingerprints.

Defendant a person accused of a crime.

Deoxyribonucleic acid (DNA) the information-carrying molecule in the cells of all organisms.

Electrophoresis a method for separating chemicals within a sample that makes use of the different sizes and differing electrical charges of different chemical molecules.

Enzyme biological molecule that increases the rate of a specific chemical reaction.

Exemplar a typical example, e.g. a sample of handwriting known to come from a particular individual that can be used to compare writing found on evidence.

Expert witness someone asked to give evidence because they have particular skills or experience that can help the judge and jury understand aspects of a trial.

Fingerprints the highly individual marks left by a person's fingers when he or she touches an object.

Forensic any work that relates to legal matters.

Genetic fingerprinting a way of analyzing a person's DNA that produces a record that is specific to that individual.

Impressed print a mark, such as a fingerprint or footmark, that has created an indentation in the surface of a piece of evidence.

Individual evidence evidence that can be linked with a high degree of certainty to a specific item or person.

Latent print marks that can only be detected when exposed with a chemical dye or powder.

LSD a drug that triggers hallucinations.

Luminol a chemical that reacts with iron found in blood cells to emit a blue light.

Mass spectrometer a machine that breaks molecules into fragments and then gives the mass of each fragment.

Neutron activation analysis a technically complex method of chemical analysis that determines what chemical elements are present in a sample.

Patent prints clearly visible prints or marks made by parts of the body or clothing.

Pathology the branch of medicine that diagnoses disease and causes of death, by analyzing body fluids and samples of cells and tissues.

Physical evidence any item that helps investigators discover what occurred at a crime scene.

Polymerase chain reaction a set of chemical reactions that can increase the amount of a genetic sample.

Postmortem the examination of a corpse in order to determine the cause of death.

Rifle a shoulder firearm that has a spiraling set of grooves inside the barrel.

Rigor mortis tension in muscles that occurs soon after a person has died.

Scanning electron microscope a machine that generates detailed 3-D images of microscopically small items. It can magnify an object by about 100,000 times.

Serology the scientific study of body fluids including blood, saliva, sweat, and semen.

Shotgun a shoulder firearm that discharges a mass of small pellets (shot) rather than a single bullet.

Spectrophotometer a scientific instrument that uses light to analyze purified samples and indicate what chemical is present.

Toxicology the study of chemicals that have harmful effects on living organisms.

Voiceprint the profile of an individual's voice used for comparison against another voice sample in an attempt to link it to that individual.

X-ray diffraction a method used to determine the chemical composition of a sample.

Picture Credits

Alamy: p. 21, 25, 32–33, 43, 45, 65, 83, 84, 89, 95, 99, 121, 122, 139, 140, 142, 146, 157, 158, 159

Allegheny County Coroner's Office: pp. 8, 9, 10, 11, 12, 14, 17, 19, 22, 46, 64, 68, 88, 98, 120, 124, 141, 143, 145

Corbis: p. 23, 53, 54, 58, 73, 81, 109, 132, 136, 151, 154, 168, 171

Getty Images: p. 36, 40–41, 59, 72, 75, 80, 93, 94, 119, 135

iStock photo p. 108

Newspix: p. 79

Rex Features: p. 39, 59, 60

Science Photo Library: pp. 21 (top and centre), 24, 26, 27, 28, 29, 44 (top), 48, 49, 50, 66, 76, 82 (top), 87, 101, 103, 126, 138 (top), 144, 156 (top), 163

TopFoto: p. 35, 56, 61, 131

Illustrations
Richard Burgess: p. 13, 18, 47, 87, 104, 105, 110–11, 115, 125, 161

Acknowledgments
The Publisher would like to thank the following for their "Day in the Life" contributions: Nicola Aryani, Marty Coyne, Dr. Frederick W. Fochtman, Robert B. Kennedy, Dr. Shaun Ladham, Dr. David Pryor, Dr. Kim Rossmo, Jane Moira Taupin.

Special thanks also to Roger Robson of Forensic Access Ltd, England.

Index

Italic page reference indicates picture captions

A
Abotway, Serena, 80
Acid bath murders, 36–37
Acid phosphate test, 89
Aging, computer simulation of, 41
Akhtar, Rangzaib, 153
Al Megrahi, Abdelbaset Ali Mohmed, 43
Andrews, Tracie, 60–61, *60*
Anthropology, forensic, 7, 74
Antibodies, 85, *85*
Armstrong, Terence, 112
Arsenic, 102, 105, 109
Ashworth, Dawn, 76
Autopsy, 7, 51, 61, 90, *104*, 105, 117, 129, 136, 145

B
Bacteria, 27, 69, 85, 108
Ballistics, 7, 28–29, 121, 129, 130, 133, 134, 168, 170
    databases, 127, 137
    firing distance, 126
    timing of shots, 128, 134
Barefoot morphology, 147
Barnes, Reynold, 137
Bell, Alexander Graham, 165
Bell, Alexander Melville, 165
Benson, Margaret and Scott, 146, 154–55
Benson, Steven, 154–55, *154*
Beradelli, Alessandro, 130
Biology, forensic, 27, 71
Bite marks, *141*, 150, 151, 152
Blood, 6, 7, 26, 81
    identifying, 84–85, *85*, 86, 92–93, 96
    information from, 27, 30, 61, *61*, 63, 65, 71, 97, 101, 105, 150, 153
    mass sampling, 77
    transfer, 88, 96
Blood spatter patterns, 7, 9, 18, 36, 51, 71, 86, 87, *87*, 168
Blood types, 23–24, 86

Bombs, 15
    automobile, 155
    Flight 103, 42–43, *43*
    Oklahoma City, 58–59, *58*
Bompard, Gabrielle, 32–33
Bone(s), 72, 74, 81, 105
Bradley, Steven, *56*, 57
Brown-Simpson, Nicole, 97
Buckland, Richard, 76–77
Bullets, 18, 28–29, 124, *124*, 128, 129, *131*, 136
    scratches on 22, *22*, 123, 130
Bundy, Ted, 150–51

C
Cartridge/shell cases, 20, 123, 124, 139, 130, *131*,134, 137, 167
Chamberlain, Michael and Lindy, 94–95
Chapman, Jessica, 62
Cho, Diane, 91
Chromatography, 30, 102, 106, 161
    gas, 28, *28*, 102
Clothing, evidence from, 71
Computer printers, 160, 161
Connally, John, 136
Coroner, role of, 6
Coyne, Marty, 90
Crime scene, 9, 10–11, *10*, *12*, *13*, *14*, 51
    documenting, 11, 142
    protocol, 11–13
    safety at, 12
Criminal intelligence analyst, 166
Crippen, Dr. Hawley Harvey, 107
Curley, Robert and Joann, 116
Curtis, Milton, 170
Cyanide poisoning, 105, 113

D
DaRonch, Carol, 150
D'Autremont brothers, 54–55, *54*
Davis, Debbie Dudley, 91
Decomposition, 19, 28
Dental evidence, 36, 74, 148, 150, *151*, 152
Devaney, Julie Anne, 149

Dingo attack, 94–95
Dixon, Derek, 137
DNA, 66
    analysis, 21, 24, *26*, 27, 30, 31, 63, 65, 67, *67*, 68–69, 87
    databases, 70
    evidence, 69, 71, 73, 75, 77, 78, 81, 129
    mitochondrial, 72
    profiling, 91, 97, 153
    retrieval, 40, *66*, 88, 89
Documentation, 11, 16, 26
    "chain of custody," 15, 26
Documents, 7, 29, 158–62
    security features on, 162
Dogs, tracking, 15, *17*
Downey, Christine, 110–11
Drugs, 30
    "date rape," 89
    detecting, 28, *28*, 102, 103, *103*
    illegal, 15, 21, *21*, 85, 100–102
    overdose, 99, 105, 106
    See also specific types
Durand-Deacon, Olivia, 36–37

E
Electrophoresis, 30, 68
Elmore, Belle, 107
Entomology, forensic, 7, 28
Epidemiology, 29
Evidence. *See also* Samples
    circumstantial, 22–24, 38
    contamination of, 16, 26
    individual, 22–24
    physical, 20–24
    preserving, 12–13
    recording, 11, 16, 26
    searching for, 14–15, 100–101
    storing, 16
    testing, 19–22
Explosives, 27, 42
    traces of, 59
Eyrand, Michael, 32–33

F
Face powder, 53
Fhimah, Al Amin Khalifa, 43
Fibers, 6, 21, 43, 46, 48–49, *49*, 62, 88, 149

Filbert, Margarethe, 52
Fingernails, evidence under, 53,
    88, *88*, 153
Fingerprints, 22, *22*, 29, 62, 93,
    113, 129, *146*, 149
    databases, 143–44, *144*, 170
    from dead body, 145
    electronic, 146
    impressed, 143
    latent, 143, 145, *145*
    mass fingerprinting, 144, 149
    patent, 143
Firearms, *122. See also* Ballistics
    evidence from, 122–28, 129
    serial numbers of, 127–28, 170
    wounds caused by, 122, *125*,
    129, 134, 168
First responder, 11–13, 140
Fisher, Larry, 73
Fochtman, Dr. Frederick W., 106
Footprints, 22, 141, 149. *See also*
    Shoeprints
    casting 140–41
Forensic nurses, 88
Forgery, 29, 117, 159
Fur, 48, *48*

G

Gamma counters, 106
Genetic fingerprint, 66, 68, *68*.
    See also DNA
Geographic profiling, 31
Geology, 26, 52
Gibbs, Eddie Lee, 137
Goddard, Calvin, 130
Goldman, Ronald, 97
Gouffé, Toussaint-Augsent,
    32–33
Gourbin, Emile, 53
Graphology. *See* Handwriting
Griffiths, Peter, 149
Grills, Caroline, 105, 110–11
Grundy, Kathleen, 117
Gunpowder, 30
Gunshot residue, 20, 21, *21*, 29,
    121, *124*, 125–26
    on suspects, 126, *126*

H

Haigh, John George, 36–37, *37*
Hair, 6, 7, 46–48, *46*, *47*, 53, 55,
    62, 65, 66, 68–69, 81, 91
    detecting chemicals in, 105,
    116
    retrieval, 47
    testing, 21, *21*, 30, 47–48
Hamilton, Alexander, 130
Handwriting, 157, 158–60, *158*,
    159, 169, 170
Harper, Lynne, 38–39
Harris, Jean, 168, *168*
Harvey, Lee, 60–61
Hay, Gordon, 152
Haydon, Elizabeth, 78
Head-space analyzers, 106
Hellems, Dr. Susan, 91
Huntley, Ian, 62
Hussong, Brian, 163, 167
Hutchinson, Arthur, 96
Hyoscine poisoning, 107

I

Image analysis software, 141, 162
Immunoassay analyzers, 106
Ink analysis, 161–62, *161*
Innocence, establishing, 69, 73
Interpol, 63, 70
Iowa, USS, 132–33, *133*

J

Jackson, Kevin, 153
Jean, Ali, 137
Jeffreys, Dr. Alec, *76*, *77*
Jin, Hyo Jung, 63
Joesbury, Andrea, 81

K

Kelly, Ian, 77
Kennedy, President John F., 136,
    136
Kennedy, Robert B., 147
Khan, Raees, 153
Kidnapping, 56–57, 171
Kim, Kyo Soo, 63
Kostov, Vladimir, 115

L

Laboratory, forensics, 25–30, *25*
Ladham, Dr. Shaun, 51
LaFeve, Neil, 163, 167
Laitner family murders, 96
Landsteiner, Karl, 86
Lane, Barry Wayne, 78
Latelle, Marie, 53
Leach, Kimberly, 150, 151
LeNeve, Ethel, 107
Levine, Dr. Lowell J., 150, *151*
Levy, Lisa, 150, *151*
List family murders, 40–41
Litvinenko, Alexander, 118–19,
    119
Locard, Dr. Edmond, 53, *53*
Lugovoi, Andrei, 118, 119
Lundberg, John and Eveline,
    110–11

M

Maggots, 28, 35, 39
Mann, Lynda, 76
Marchal, Ghislaine, 169
Markov, Georgi, 114–15
Marks and impressions, 7, 139,
    140–42
Marsh, James, 102, 109
Mason, Gerald, 170
Mass spectrometry, 28, 48, 102,
    106
McVeigh, Timothy, 59, *59*
Mengele, Dr. Josef, 74–75
Mickelson, Christina and Mary
    Ann, 110
Milgaard, David, 69, 73
Miller, Gail, 73
Miller, Dr. Harold, 112
Mitchell, Artie, 128, 134–35
Mitchell, James, 128,
    134–35, *135*
Morphine, 103, 105, 106, 117

N

Nails, 105, 116. *See also*
    Fingernails
Neutron activation analysis, 30,
    126, 136
Nicholas II, Tsar, 72

Nichols, Terry, 59
Nickell, Bruce and Stella, 113
Norwood, Turner, 137

O
O'Shea, Larry, 57
Oswald, Lee Harvey, 136

P
Paint, 27, 30, 50, *50*, 63
Palm Beach shootings, 137
Palm prints, 146, 155
PanAm Flight 103, 42–43, *43*
Papin, Georgina, 81
Parkman, Dr. George, 148
Parmenter, Frederick, 124, 130
Paternity, establishing, 69
Pathologist, forensic, 6, 51, 90,
    105, 122
Peacock, Linda, 152
Peck, Mr. and Mrs. John, 108–109
Phillips, Richard, 170
Photography, forensic, 15, 28, 90,
    141, 142, *142*, 143
Physical science unit, 26–27
Pickton, Robert "Willie," 80–81
Piggy Palace murders, 80–81
Pitchfork, Colin, 77
Poison(s), 7, 28, 99, 105, 106
    See also specific types
Politovskaya, Anna, 118
Pollen, 27, 62
Polonium-210 poisoning, 118
Popp, Georg, 52
Postmortem. *See* Autopsy
Pryor, Dr. David, 129
Psychological profiling, 31

R
Raddad, Omar, 169
Rape, 38, 47, 67, 71, 73, 76,
    88–89, 91, 166, 170
Reconstruction, crime, 7, 18, *18*
    computer simulation, 15
Reconstruction, facial, 40, 41
Reso, Sidney, 171
Ricin poisoning, 114–15
Rogerson, Mary, 34–35
Rossmo, Dr. Kim, 31
Russian imperial family, 72, *72*
Ruxton, Dr. Buck, 34–35
Ruxton, Isabella, 34–35, *35*

S
Sacco, Nicola, 124, 130–31
Saliva, 6, 65
Samples.
    analyzing, 30
    biological, 27
    comparing, 20–21
    identifying, 20
    See also specific substances
Scaramella, Mario, 118
Scanning electron microscope,
    126–27
Scene of crime. *See* Crime scene
Schlicher, Andreas, 52
Schmidt, Johann, 92
Seale, Arthur and Jackie, 171
Seconal poisoning, 112
Semen, 6, 30, 66, 67, 71, 73, 81,
    88, 91
    retrieving, 89
Serology, 7, 27
Sexual assault, 88–89, 149
Shipman, Dr. Harold, 105, 117
Shoeprints, 141, 142
Shotguns, *125*, 126
Signatures, 158, 159
Simpson, O.J., 97
Skin, 53, 65, 116, 153
Snow, Susan, 113
Snowtown Monstrosities, 78–79
Soham murders, 62
Soil(s), 27, 30, 52
Song, In Hea, 63
South Side Rapist, 66, 91
Spectrograph, light, 164
    sound, 164, 165, 167
Spectrometry, 30
Spectrophotometry, 48, 126
Spencer, Timothy, 91
Spilsbury, Sir Bernard, 107
Stomach contents, 105, 109, 112
Stubbe, Hermann and Peter,
    92–93
Suicide, 125
Suspects, handling of, 16–17,
    126, *126*

T
Tarnower, Dr. Herman, 168
Taupin, Jane Moira, 71
Telephone calls, 128, 134, 163,
    165, 171

Tessnow, Ludwig, 92–93
Thallium poisoning, 105,
    110–11, *111*, 116
Thomas, Angeline, 110
Thorne, Graeme, 56–57
Tire tracks, 140, 142
Tool marks, 16, 142, 153
Toxicology, forensic, 27–28, *28*,
    99, 101–105, *101*, 106, 116
Trace evidence, 6, 7, 21, 27, 57, 85
Tresize, Clinton Douglas, 78
Truscott, Steven, 38–39, *39*
Tucker, Susan, 91
Turner, Larry, 137
Typewriter script, 160–61

U
Uhlenhuth, Paul,
    92–93, *93*
Umbrella gun, 114, *115*
Union Pacific mail train
    murders, 54–55
Urine, 85, 89, *89*, 101, 105, 106,
    118

V
Vanzetti, Bartolomeo, 130–31
Vehicle identification, 58
Victim identity, establishing,
    32, 34–35, 36–37, 63, 69, 72,
    78, 107
Video images, 15, 74
Viruses, 69, 85
Vlassakis, James, 78, 79
Voiceprint analysis, 157, 163–65,
    166
Voice production, 164

W
Waite, Dr. Arthur Warren, 102,
    108–109, *109*
Warren Commission, 136
Webster, Dr. John, 148
Wells, Holly, 62
Wilson, Mona, *80*, 81
Witness statements, 17, 18
Wolfe, Brenda, 81

Z
Zaman, Rashad, 153